Auditing Breast Cancer Care

by

Asad Salman: Consultant Surgeon,
West Sussex Breast Centre at Worthing Hospital;

Anand Kumar: Head of School of Health Studies
Chichester Institute of Higher Education;

Lorna Tomblin: Clinical Trial Co-ordinator,
West Sussex Breast Centre at Worthing Hospital.

Foreword by
Prof. Michael Baum

Second Edition

AENEAS PRESS

Table of Contents

Foreword   vii
Acknowledgements   ix

Chap 1
What is Audit all about?   2
some definitions of audit   2
summary of criteria of audit   10
summary of use and value of audit   14
some case studies of audit   17
origins of Audit in the NHS   24

Chap 2
Audit in context of an emerging research
    based culture in the NHS   29
the NHS & Community Care Act
    stipulation on research   34
the role of auditing in the new health service
    with respect to evidence based medicine   37
summary of EBM movement   38
reflection on practice   40

Chap 3
methodology   46
cohort 1   47
cohort 2   48
stage 1 data gathering procedures   48
stage 2 data gathering procedures   49
stage 3 data gathering procedures   49
spreadsheet headings   50

Chap 4

Data analysis	53
intitial consideration	53
number of patients in the two cohorts	54
consequences of volume for workload	59
further analysis on the number of patients seen	60
age characteristics of the two cohorts	61
some questions to reflect upon in respect of age characteristics	62
practice implications	63
last seen date	63
survival period	64
incidence of breast cancer in south Thames region	64
tumour categories	65
size of tumours in mms	67
grade of tumours	67
nodes positive	68
on treatment approaches	69
questions in respect of variations in treatment	72
survival issues	72
on affected sides	74
interval data	74
on death and mortality	75
summary of audit findings	76

Chap 5

Lessons learnt from the conduct of the audit	77
on the nature and value of psychological support	79
implications of audit workload	82
reflection on symptomatic and screen detected patients	83
on the notion of follow up	83
reflections on the management of breast cancer	84
reflections on professional development through reflective practice and audit	87

Appendices	89
References/Bibliography	103
Index	107

Foreword

by
Professor Michael Baum

Anyone who heard me deliver the Ernest Miles Lecture at the Royal College of Surgeons on Thursday the 27th November 1997 might be surprised to see that I am writing a foreword to a book entitled "Auditing Breast Cancer Care". I concluded my lecture by stating that after more than thirty years in clinical research on the natural history and management of breast cancer, I now wanted to step down and pass on the baton to the new generation of young Consultant surgeons. Yet I was hesitant to do so, because listening to so many of them holding forth on the importance of "guidelines" and "audit", I wondered where the visionaries had gone, as without vision there is unlikely to be any progress.

One can even imagine what an audit meeting might have been like thirty years ago at a time when the concept was not yet fashionable. The surgical masters would have insisted that all women with early breast cancer must have a Halsted radical mastectomy and that at least twenty five lymph nodes would have been removed and subjected to histological sectioning and castigated those who accidentally cut across lymphatic planes. Such audit would have guaranteed the technical perfection of the surgical procedure but the same number of women would have continued to die of breast cancer to this day.

Fortunately thirty years ago there were men of vision who challenged the underlying paradigm and established randomised controlled trials that demonstrated the equivalence of breast conserving techniques and the superiority of adjuvant systemic therapy over a policy of waiting and watching for the distant metastases to announce themselves.

Of course having got this far, it would indeed be foolish to ignore audit which at least ensures that all these hard learnt lessons are being implemented on a day to day basis so that the best outcomes are available to all women in the UK and treatment is no longer a lottery. So we can see that audit alone is not sufficient nor a Society of swash buckling visionary surgeons all doing their own thing. It is the beauty of this little book to demonstrate that the best features of clinical audit in fact incorporate and encourage the best features of clinical research and clinical accountancy.

Thus on page 29, the authors emphasise the philosophical approaches to audit and research and demonstrate later on in the text that the best type of audit generates hypotheses that can later be tested using the deductive process in clinical trials. In the section, "reflection on practice", it is emphasised that mere reflection without a structure will take us nowhere with the constant danger of our observations being interpreted in a way that reinforces ones' prejudice. True reflection on practice has to be self critical with a culture where every observation is teased in a way that may challenge our most cherished beliefs.

As the best evidence that the authors are not merely paying lip service to these beliefs, we learn that central to their methodology and a key person in their data gathering within the unit is a Clinical Trials Co-ordinator. Her role in addition, to maintaining the database and extracting information for data analysis is also to ensure that all suitable patients are entered into clinical trials. An outcome measure of the success of the Centre is the percentage of suitable patients who are in fact entered into clinical trials or to quote from page 53, "in this way we will demonstrate how audit can be used to instigate and inform ongoing empirical work".

The latter part of the book demonstrates examples of what can be learnt from audit providing some fascinating vignettes and leading to some challenging conclusions. For example looking at their two major sets of data coming from a symptomatic and screen detected cancers, the authors are confidently able to recommend that follow up care could be shared with general practitioners without any consequential reduction in the quality of outcome. Furthermore the analysis of pathological subtypes and survival experience comparing screen detected and the symptomatic population once again emphasises the hazards of lead times bias and length bias when trying to interpret the benefits of mammographic screening.

Finally, their very respectable level of an interval cancer rate suggests that unlike much published data so far, their performance is compatible with a significant reduction in breast cancer specific mortality and this must surely be due to the diagnostic acumen of the radiologists involved in the programme.

This modest but important book is published to co-incide with the opening of a purpose built breast Centre to serve West Sussex. The women in that area can therefore be assured that should they develop breast symptoms the accuracy of their diagnosis, the appropriateness of their treatment and their opportunity to join clinical trials at the cutting edge of the subject will no longer be a lottery.

Acknowledgments

This book has been made possible through the combined efforts of a number of individuals. We would like to thank the many colleagues who have contributed to the audit project, from the initial years of data collection, right through to the conception of this book. It is not possible to name every individual at Worthing Hospital. We would however like to thank the following: Mr G W Arthur, former Consultant Surgeon who encouraged data collection; Mr G Dickson, Consultant Surgeon & Mr A Johri, Staff Grade Surgeon; Dr D C Cooper who was involved as Consultant Pathologist at the beginning, Consultant Pathologists Dr K Roberts, Dr Susan Davies, Dr Karen Blessing and Dr J Grant assisted by Liz Berry, Senior MLSO, with her colleagues in cytology and histopathology.

A vital component has been the contribution of Paula Rabin and the mammographic radiographers led by Dr Anne Hubbard and Dr Linda Rockall, Consultant Radiologists. The operating theatre staff have obviously been involved and formed a capable team from the outset, with a special contribution by the team leader Pat Scott.

The specialist breast care nurses have also been involved and we would like to thank in particular Helen Brassington, Serena Streatfield, Beryl Bird, Eileen Gough, Elizabeth Toon, Lin Hall & Judith Finlay. We also acknowledge the sterling efforts of our support groups who have raised much needed funds to support some of this work and in particular Trish Silcock.

Acknowledgement is also due to the contributions made by Janet Ansell and Pam Stuart-Jones, Breast Screening Unit, St. Lukes Hospital, Guildford, for their support and patience in supplying copies of pathology reports and listings of breast cancers, seen at Worthing Hospital and privately. This has contributed enormously to the quality of the audit data. Above all, we would like to express our gratitude to Dr G Deutsch, Dr V Svoboda, Dr G Khoury, Dr C Topham, Dr S Murrell, Dr M Wilkins and all their teams at the Oncology Centres.

We also acknowledge the valuable help that a number of other colleagues have provided towards the publication. Tessa Neighbour painstakingly input the data onto SPSS and we are grateful for the help that she provided. Joan Stephens from the Faculty of Science at Chichester Institute of Higher Education has listened to discussions and has commented on matters statistical. Dr Gill Kester from the School of Health Studies has proof read final drafts. Peter Mullans at Technical Graphics and St. Richards Press transformed the manuscript to an inspiring layout. Linda Grant and Stephen Palmer from ZENECA Pharma, have provided much needed support towards the conception of this project. Finally, we are indebted to Prof Michael Baum who has commented upon two drafts of the manuscript and who has written the foreword of the book.

Whilst the help and support that we have derived has been beneficial in more ways than one, we are finally responsible for omissions and errors, if any.

Chapter 1

This chapter deals with a number of central issues. We will discuss the definitions, principles and practice of audit. Based upon this, we will then report on an audit study of two cohorts of breast cancer patients.

Audit has a fundamental role to play in gathering data that can be analysed to evaluate clinical practice. In addition, we believe that it is a useful tool for the development of a research based culture and as such we aim to establish the link between audit and research .

A number of professional issues underpin the use of audit in clinical practice. These include a desire to improve practice by gathering data to evaluate outcomes and to identify ways to save on costs. The conduct of audit therefore presupposes a wish to improve professional practice. The essential attribute of "reflection on practice" which involves actions, including those of identifying and learning from the lessons derived from practice, is one which is vital to the successful audit. We submit that this breast cancer audit demonstrates the link between reflective practice and research. In this way, we are extending the scope of audit to demonstrate how it can enhance professional development, practice and research. Finally, in keeping with one of the fundamental roles of audit, we intend to reflect on our own practice and to show how the audit study has enabled us to inform and change the way in which we practice.

In order to address the above issues, we need to establish the major role that audit serves in action based research. We must first consider the links between audit and clinical practice. A number of questions need addressing and include:-

- What is audit all about?
- What are its origins in the NHS?
- What purposes does it serve?
- What role does it serve in Breast Cancer Care?

We propose to deal with these issues in order. As we are establishing a case for reflective practice in surgical care through the medium of our audit study, we intend to discuss these points in detail. We will examine the theoretical and policy issues that relate to each of these items. We intend to provide a robust discussion of these concepts so that clinicians could use, develop and apply them in a manner appropriate to their own specialities.

What is audit all about?

Audit, as a clinical tool, is based upon a number of fundamental considerations. We have already stated that it can be incorporated in a strategy for developing research based practice. In particular it provides on-going data that can influence practice and policy. Audit can serve several stakeholders including clinicians. Currently, it is also seen as a process of establishing a cost effective health service. For instance, work carried out by Aspley (1996) demonstrated how audit has been used as a basis of developing quality assurance in a Radiotherapy Centre, thus implementing ISO 9002 in cancer care. A number of cases describing the variety of ways in which audit has been deployed has recently been appearing in the clinical and professional literature, with a good deal of frequency.

Some definitions of Audit

Davies et al (1996) defined audit as the "systematic critical analysis of the quality of medical care, including the procedures used for diagnosis and treatment, use of resources and the resulting outcome and quality of life for patients". They perceived it as a powerful tool and method of monitoring change and raising standards. In this study, Davies et al were able to demonstrate varying levels of commitment to the use of audit amongst a sample of general practitioner surgeries.

Audit is defined as "an official examination of"
Concise Oxford dictionary

Chambers Everyday Paperback dictionary provides a definition which regards audit as "an examination of accounts by one or more duly authorised persons"

Gordon (1994) asserts that the focus of audit is on "a limited set of significant, measurable and monitorable indicators by which clinical practice is given a set of cases/episodes that can be measured against a qualitative norm".

Buxton (1994) asserted that audit is now seen by many "as an inherently good thing; it is an activity that by definition deserves support and encouragement".

Williams (1996) argues that the word "audit has more traditional meanings for surgeons and is used in a variety of ways". For instance, he suggested that audit has a variety of roles in related activities, as is indicated below:-

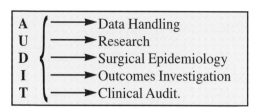

A	⟶ Data Handling
U	⟶ Research
D	⟶ Surgical Epidemiology
I	⟶ Outcomes Investigation
T	⟶ Clinical Audit.

He goes on to suggest that seen in this way audit can be differentiated from research in that:-

"Research seeks to discover new information;
am I singing the right song?
Audit seeks to improve health care;
am I singing the song right?"

The elements of clinical audit can be separated into:-

- development of an audit tool
- audit of other professions
- audit of own health care practice,
  sometimes referred to as process audit

The NHS Executive and Greenhalgh and Company Ltd (1996) proposed that the Audit process is about the monitoring of *"progress towards the targets or standards which may be informed by national guidance which may have resulted in the development of protocols which describe how the processes should be expected to be carried out"*.

They suggested that *"audit is not an end in itself, rather it is carried out with the expectation that the current situation may need to change. This implies that the current situation must first be defined and any beneficial practices should be documented as guidance for the future"*.

It was further proposed by these workers that any topic that can be defined and measured could be the focus of an audit. Several examples have been put forward as issues that may benefit from audit. One case cited included that of "the evaluation of treatment of an individual by a peer group of professionals or as part of the assessment of the effect of revised processes and procedures on clinical outcomes".

Some of the essential elements that are recognised as vital to the development of an effective audit programme include :-

"ensuring that all health care practitioners have a shared vision of audit and its importance"

"establishing consensus on what could be and what should be audited"

"agreeing the priority of audit relative to other calls on time and resources"

"determining the evaluation protocol for the audit activity itself"

"giving consideration on how organisational attitudes and approach can be expected to change as a result of the application of the general principles of audit"

"encouraging the development of team work and relationships between management and clinical staff to cultivate a positive joint commitment to audit initiatives".

Robinson (1996) argued that the history of medical audit and of audit used in nursing and professions supplementary to medicine has been closely intertwined in the development of quality assurance (QA) systems. For the most part QA was introduced by the professional bodies to initiate "national standards" in respect of a wide range of aspects of care, though by no means comprehensively so.

The Department of Health (DoH) provided the impetus for the uptake of audit through pump priming initiatives to develop medical audit in a number of pilot sites. Subsequently, support was provided for the uptake of audit in nursing and the therapy professions.

Initially, the introduction of audit and medical audit in particular was motivated by professional as well as by DoH concerns. For the most part this was promoted by individual enthusiasts. On the other hand, non-medical audit was usually seen as being motivated by managerial involvement. Medical, as well as other professional audits are now superseded by a more broadly focused approach. Current practice is one in which a range of professional and other interests combine efforts to audit practice, collectively.

Despite the initial impetus and support for promoting audit, uptake and development have been slow. A number of studies have attempted to explore the factors contributing to this situation and to account for why participation and involvement have been low. These studies point to a range of constraints. For instance, Firth-Cozens and Storer (1992) identified a lack of time and guidance as factors explaining low uptake. Kerrison, Packwood and Buxton (1993) suggested that lack of authority to implement and act upon audit findings was seen as a problem in their study. Thompson and Barton (1994) indicated that concerns about the confidential nature of audit data and findings temper enthusiasm for the use of such findings.

Robinson (1996) demonstrated that in her own study located at some 6 hospital trusts, over 100 single and multi-professional audit studies were being conducted on service delivery/quality/resource and organisational issues. The constraints of audit identified earlier are not insurmountable, as the volume of recent audit activity across a variety of specialisms would demonstrate. A major factor towards enhancing audit activity is that of integrating audit and evaluation into the everyday practice of health care professionals.

The NHS Executive and Greeenhalgh & Co (1996) outline a number of essential principles of audit as follows:-

- *audit should be an accepted routine part of the practice and not an ad hoc exercise which may be viewed with suspicion;*
- *audit should be led by appropriate professionals and should consider the views of all third parties;*
- *audit should be informed by all relevant data, whatever the sources, and where systems providing the data are not integrated, the data should be collated for analysis of the full picture;*
- *the focus, whenever feasible, should be on outcomes; though some clinicians feel that process audits are also important and perhaps more achievable;*
- *the results of audit and the audit processes which provided satisfactory results, should themselves inform future education and training in the subject of the audit, in addition to informing developments in clinical practice;*
- *audit targets should be set and agreed within a local context, taking account of any relevant national or professional standards or guidance which exists.*
- *audit should inform both operational and strategic planning.*

Audit, then, is perceived as a mechanism or "means of monitoring" that progress is being made towards targets set in a particular situation. But as is indicated above, there are a number of elements and processes that make audit a complex activity, with potentially several outcomes.

Based on a synthesis of views and perspectives of audit, one can deduce a common framework of the audit process. Some workers defined this as an audit cycle; others talk in terms of an audit spiral.

Fig 1. adapted from NHS Executive and Greenhalgh and Co.(1996)

A Model of Audit

The Audit Cycle

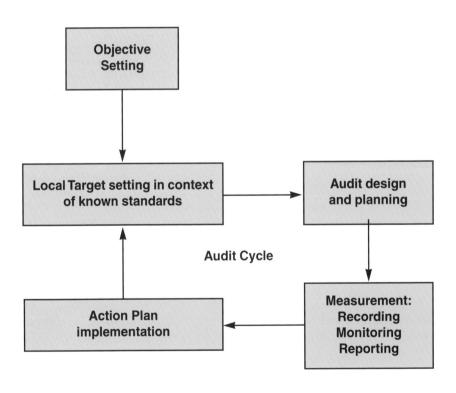

It is apparent from this schematisation that audit therefore includes a series of well defined phases and activities which can be summarised as follows:-

Phase	Action required
setting objectives	this phase involves the formulation of objectives which have been agreed by appropriate professionals and staff involved in the audit study. These objectives will benefit from thorough consultation of the relevant literature and with personnel involved
standard setting	this will need to be anchored to national standards as well locally accepted arrangements and agreements
audit design and planning	this phase may benefit from previously conducted work in order to help in the design and development which will build on previous findings
measurement, recording, monitoring, reporting	this phase is at the base of data gathering and data analysis. It is a methodical approach to data gathering which makes effective use of information systems, patient data bases and other diagnostic and treatment outcome measures.
implementation phase	requires a systematic consideration of all sources used in measurement stage to determine current progress
completing the cycle	may lead to realignment or change of practice; furthermore, outcomes may lead to an ongoing audit as well as publication of findings.

The other view of audit is that which regards it as a spiral process as described by Kumar and Brown (1992). Here audit is regarded in a similar manner to action based research in which "implementation of actions for change and review usually produce progress towards the stated level of quality".

They suggested that audit can be seen as a process which has the effect of "continually improving quality". They described this as the audit spiral as it allows for evaluation, comparison and change in a cyclical manner towards the raising of standards.

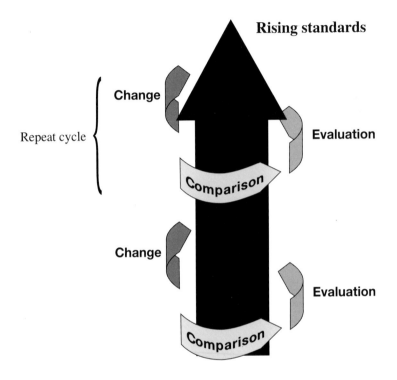

Audit, as it is commonly practised, has only recently been adopted by the NHS. It was first used in 1952 in connection with the enquiry into maternal deaths. With the Griffiths driven reforms and in particular Working for Patients, greater emphasis was placed on persuading medical practitioners to make more systematic use of audit as an integral aspect of practice. The intention was that practitioners could make use of peer review as a basis of developing skills and expertise of value in the conduct of audit. The basis of medical audit was therefore seen to be patient focused and to some extent multi-dimensional in terms of considering diagnosis, treatment, care interventions and follow up. The emphasis on medical rather than clinical aspects, may serve to indicate that the onus was on medical staff. In effect, data gathered were derived mainly by the efforts of other practitioners and adminstrative staff.

As we have seen earlier, attempts to explore definitions and meanings of audit are typified by wide variation. It is generally conceded that the term audit means different things to different people. Moreover, it is used in a variety of ways. For instance, usage and reference covers several facets including:

- audit

- clinical audit

- medical audit.

From this, it is obvious that there are a number of important considerations in the making of a successful audit study. Some workers identify the need for establishing criteria at the outset. We intend to revisit these criteria later. There are however, a number of essential processes that can be identified.

First, it is essential that audit is recognised as a central plank of the work of the unit or organisation. In addition, those involved must understand the key principles of audit. We have referred to these earlier.

Second, successful audits require the drive of a "champion" whose task is to provide leadership, motivation and overall co-ordination of the respective stages /phases of the study. Some workers regard champions to be a vital link to all involved in the audit. They command respect and ensure sensitivity which enable them to act upon the applications and measurements derived from the audit. Like most processes, the successful outcome of an initial audit may impact on perceptions and attitudes on future and on-going audits.

Third, as has been established earlier, a need exists for clear and explicit goals and measurable targets which are effectively communicated and understood. Additionally as the audit may be multi-layered, drawing from a number of applications and professionals, it is vital that adequate time for communication and interaction is allowed for.

Fourth, it is essential that topics identified for audit are those which are amenable to change. As we have established previously, audit should be underlined by its capacity to change practice.

Fifth, key personnel from a variety of backgrounds must be involved centrally in the conduct of the audit. The role that each fulfils should be distinct in contributing to the overall success of the audit.

Finally the need to access multiple data sources cannot be overstated. Data derived from one audit can be compared with other sources and findings, allowing further analysis to be carried out.

Summary of key criteria of audit :-

- ensure understanding of the principles of audit
- use a champion to harness and motivate team
- establish clear and achievable goals
- choose topics judiciously
- involve key personnel and promote ownership
- access many data sources

As far as central government is concerned, audit is here to stay and is championed by the National Audit Office. Scott (1989) provided an account which showed three distinct ways of interpreting the term.

First, he suggests that audit is "concerned with an analysis of the resources and equipment required for a particular task". This kind of perspective represents an interpretation that is used by accountants, and to some extent economists, in estimating and projecting cost. In this way, provision can be made to ensure that adequate resources are available to ensure the viability of the service in the first instance. This method also allows for detecting changes or trends in the way services are used.

The **second** interpretation identified is that in which audit is used to assess the extent to which resources are utilised appropriately. Here, emphasis is placed on cost effectiveness or equitable distribution across different parts of the country. A number of stakeholders, including purchasers of health services, may be keenly interested in analysis of this kind. Dennis (1994) suggested that in the rapidly developing internal market, this kind of purchaser intelligence is vital as a baseline in the negotiation of contracts with providers. Here, then, one can identify a use of audit which is related to the concept of service effectiveness.

The **third** perspective suggested by Scott is that used by doctors and is a "methodology for continuing medical education which is concerned with defining the quality of services and with facilitating the process of change". To distinguish it from the other two perspectives, it is usually regarded as medical audit. This particular aspect is being promoted by the Royal Colleges. To some extent it is conceptually linked to the recently introduced movement of evidence based practice. Scott suggests that medical audit can be conceptualised as a circular process.

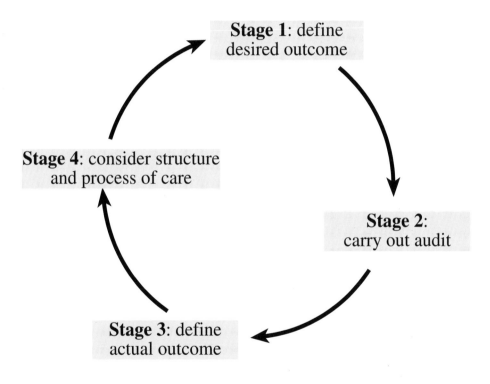

It brings participants back to the beginning with the insight to view their tasks from a different perspective and to raise the quality of care they provide.

Crombie et al (1992) reiterated the views of Mckee et al (1989) and Shaw (1990a) who argue that "audit includes a range of activities from review of individual cases to multi-centre data collection on thousands of patients" (page 182). The emphasis alluded to here is primarily that of data gathering and analysis across variable sample sizes. Whereas, in past years, audit was carried out solely by enthusiasts, now it is evident that everyone is collecting data, as within the new and emergent culture of the health service, everybody is supposed to be collecting it. The reality is that although there is much more time spent on data gathering, the data sources and methods used vary enormously. As a consequence the audit derived thus may serve local needs, but contributes little to multi centre evaluation studies.

Such difficulty in making comparisons has naturally led some, including Baker (1990), Moss and Smith (1991) and Crombie et al (1992), to argue that audit studies are not "as effective as they could be". Whilst others, such as Shaw and Costain (1989) and Baker (1990), have indicated a need for an "audit of audit" it is arguable whether such a meta-review is possible, given the different starting points of such studies in the first place. One therefore needs to reflect more intently on the dynamics of audit. Those developing and using audit need to understand the basic complexity associated with framing and adopting audit in practice. Additionally, they also need to have knowledge of the ways in which such complexities could be minimised.

Smith (1990) asserts that audit "is most often described in terms of a cycle involving an assessment of the effects of any changes". Here, emphasis seems to be placed on the importance of evaluation that audit provides. He goes on to suggest that the most convincing audits are those that report or demonstrate progressive improvements in services or care provided. In this way audit is seen as a cyclical process in which current practice or care is observed or measured. This is then compared against standards agreed or specified alongside established criteria. Findings and outcomes are then acted upon to refine practice. The similarity here between action based learning derived from the work of Revans (1980) and action based research cannot be overstated and we will develop this theme further in Chapter 2.

There are two interesting and useful accounts on audit which the reader may wish to consult. The papers by Crombie et al (1992) and Williams (1996) are immensely useful. Crombie et al discuss the construction of audit by asking essential questions that are central to the development of any data collection exercise.

The three simple questions are:-

- why was it done?
- how was it done?
- what did it find?

To this, one can add other questions assuming that one is starting from the other end; ie the developmental end. In such a situation other relevant questions may include:-

- what does one need to collect data on and with what precision?
- who are the major/minor stakeholders involved in such data gathering?
- how are the data found to be used ?

Crombie et al's three simple questions allow us to engage with audit in a meaningful and purposeful manner not previously considered. For instance, the *"why"* was it done type question " applies to the reason for selecting a topic for investigation as well as the objectives of the study". The *"how"* type question enables us to reflect upon "all the facets of the methods used to achieve those objectives". Similarly *"what"* type questions "afford the opportunity to interpret the findings and consider their implications". Evidently the onus is on audit users to reflect on and develop a deeper understanding of the tools used in audits. Evaluation of outcomes and implications for the services provide one with opportunities to close the loop. ie to develop an audit tool and make it effective and worthwhile for the service, users and sponsors alike. The process may at face value appear simple but it requires a good deal of organisational ease to make it work effectively.

"Why" type questions are about the aim of the audit. Most of us would agree that the essential purpose of using audits is to improve the quality of health care. Others would add to this by incorporating issues on service planning, resource utilisation and cost accounting. Crombie at al suggest that the latter of these concerns are not within the scope of audit and as such should be verified by other means. This is debatable, as it is likely that data collection is founded on this imperative; ie are we using resources effectively, if not, why not and then how can improvements be made?

Summary of use and value of audit

	Item	Desirable features	Adverse Features
the why type questions	purpose	simple and clearly stated primarily aimed at audit intention to effect change	diffuse, general data collection service planning resource management, or cost accounting observe practice only
	selection of topic	well reasoned	reasons not stated
the how type questions	setting of standards	set prior to study objective criteria justified target stated	no standards set subjective criteria no justification target unstated
	method	simplest for purpose only essential data collected suitable sample size BMJ statistical checklist met possibility of bias considered	more complex than necessary much unused data collected sample size ignored not met bias ignored
The what type questions	interpretation	deficiency of care recognised specific solutions proposed educational impact appreciated	current practice vindicated solutions not considered, or only general ones proposed ignored
	effecting change	planned programme of change all staff involved active feedback audit evaluated	no change attempted top down or enthusiasts only passive feedback no evaluation of changes.

There are however, numerous other accounts which can be called upon to elucidate the nature of audits. The NHSE and Greenhalgh and Company Limited (1996) assert that where clinical audit is used, and used effectively for that matter, a number of benefits can accrue. They suggest for instance that audit protocols can have a significant effect on :-

> *"the actual use of proven good practices to the benefit of direct patient care"*
> *"the avoidance of repeat audits through ignorance of previous work"*
> *"the increased use of proven practice in professional education"*
> *"the enhancement of the effectiveness of open learning by making guidance available for reference to the operational clinical workstation"*

Whilst it is obvious that these benefits can accrue when and where audit protocols are well established and developed, it is clear that a number of other considerations come to the fore. For instance, clinical audit needs to be integrated with the wider cultural processes of the unit or department as a fully developed strategy rather than as an end itself.

It is essential to start by determining clearly the information that should be gathered as there is the potential to include too much. Guidelines for selecting items for auditing are available and the work of Shaw (1990a), Garvigan (1996) and the British Breast Group (1994) as well as BASO (1994) are all cases in point. The final arbiter in the selection of items should be considerations about the value of the activity in enabling decisions about clinical effectiveness. Crombie at al assert that the "chosen activity should be clinical importance because it is common, high risk or high cost" (page 182). Whatever areas or topics are chosen, it is paramount that they are explicitly defined, focused and are amenable to bench marking or standard setting.

Questions about how audits are conducted have been well addressed by a number of sources, most of which recognise the problematic nature of methodologies used. A common problem is that data gathered are collated without recourse to the purpose and methods by which the data will be analysed. In this manner some of the initial pre-requisites for determining "how data are gathered and as to how standards are set" are usually overlooked. Writers including Donabedian (1988) and Shaw (1990b) have recognised standard setting as a difficult stage in audit and one which is not usually the starting point of an audit study.

It is important when constructing audits that adequate attention is directed to thinking about standards as the concept has varying levels of meaning. For instance, standards on the one hand may convey a meaning of what is acceptable i.e. a criterion component whilst on the other, it may represent specifications of an acceptable target i.e. the number of cases in which care is at least this good. This level of distinctiveness is borne out in the example of the audit study conducted by Kemple and Hayter in 1991. In this study the criterion standard was achievement of blood glucose levels of less than 10 mmol/litre in insulin dependent diabetic patients. The target set was 90% of patients meeting the requirement.

In all cases, criteria set in audit studies should be objective i.e. it should be measurable and or verifiable. In some cases, this is easier said than done as objective measures such as outcomes do not convey anything about quality. One way around this kind of limitation is to consider alternatives such as clinical judgement, allowing questions as to the satisfactory nature or otherwise of the treatment. Crombie et al refer to this kind of evidence, which can be seen as an alternative to objective criteria, as implicit. Whilst in principle, clinical judgement would seem to offer us something else, it is nonetheless based on a good deal of bias or subjective interpretations. Similarly, targets set should also be realistic i.e. the number of patients seen in a given time frame. Far too often, studies either fail to specify targets or simply do so as an after thought.

Whatever method one adopts at carrying out an audit study will depend on a host of considerations. McKee et al (1989) identify a range of methods that could be used depending on the circumstances in which one finds oneself. However, whatever the approach used, it is necessary that the method is appropriate and that one takes due consideration of questions of sample size, techniques of data analysis and of the issue of bias. Sackett (1979) listed some 56 sources of bias that can impact on medical research. Of particular importance here is the issue of sample selection, as in most cases , subjects in these studies are self selecting.

We have indicated that the *"why"* and the *"how"* questions are important starting points in approaching audit. But then so are the *"what"* type of concerns. The present emphasis on evidence based medicine and concerns for efficiency gains and effectiveness make*"what"* type questions somewhat superfluous, as it is possible to conjecture that all aspects of care at one time or another will be the subject of audit and evaluation. Macro issues self select and in the internal market may be essential, given the extent to which standard specifications are now becoming the basis of the contracting process between purchasers and providers. Problems of *"what"* type considerations actually relate to the gathering of information vital to the conduct of a successful audit.

Williams (1996) has similarly made an important contribution to our understanding of audit. His paper has gained the endorsement of the Director of Audit of the Royal College of Surgeons (Devlin 1996). It carries the weight of authority and is seen as confirmation of a valuable framework of relevance to the clinical community. As noted previously, Williams has argued that when assessed against its conventional basis, the word audit has "more traditional meanings for surgeons", and not surprisingly, is used in a variety of different ways.

In context of breast cancer audit, this poses a raft of problems as the kinds of data sets collated vary enormously. Despite publications of several guidelines as to what constitute essential data sets for breast cancer care, there remains substantial variation and inconsistency in practice. The recent efforts of national bodies resulting in the recommendations of protocols, including those of the BBG and BASO, may contribute towards the alleviation of some of the problems relating to non-standardisation of protocols.

Of course, as we have indicated earlier, the widespread adoption of audit allows for several distinct and separate ways in which it can be developed, used or analysed. Furthermore, we contend that this plurality of meaning and approach does allow for diverse use of audit. However, this could be seen as a double edged sword for some such as Reid (1994) have argued that this variability in approach renders comparisons and evaluation useless. In terms of learning from experience though, it is possible to argue that diversity is good in that it allows for a broad and rich seam of applications, that can benefit reflective practice and ultimately, research.

Some case studies of audit in use in surgical practice

A perusal of the literature indicates a growing body of studies in which practitioners are adopting audit as a means of developing their practice. In this section, we wish to highlight a few of these studies to indicate the range of work being carried out in surgery.

Curley et al (1996) recognised the importance of audit to their practice by asserting "that the power of surgical audit lies in the ability to clearly record complications and to compare case mix from year to year and between centres in order to compare results". They echoed the importance of "accurate data about surgical activity" as being vital for the development of new services. Data collection both in terms of its fundamental nature as well as its accuracy are seen as vital towards the establishment of meaningful audit.

In their study, which is an audit of the activity and workload of surgeons in a vascular surgical services over a 52 week period, they gathered data on:-

- number of admissions
- elective and emergency surgery
- Intermediate Equivalent Value (IEV) activity (operations per week)
- plus surgical workloads

These values were then compared with figures of recommendations of surgical workload. Their analysis indicated that workload carried out was far greater than the ideal proposed. The audit was used as evidence to justify the case for resource planning, both in terms of reorganising the surgical services as well as in making bids for additional consultant posts. This example illustrates the value of data, using locality based audit findings, to change the basis of everyday clinical practice. Curley et al concluded that audit used in this manner provides a justification for "on-going" prospective data collection in surgical practice.

In an audit study on patients undergoing surgical procedures of the parotid gland, Deans et al (1995) gathered data on 92% of all patients who had surgical treatment in this speciality over a 4 year period. The audit focused on symptom presentation, range of investigations carried out, treatment approaches and complications experienced. The retrospective nature of the audit enabled the clinicians to examine in detail, efficacy of diagnosis and treatment. They concluded that, based on a "small series with follow up", the data indicate that diseases of the parotid can be managed by general surgeons with an interest in the field. The study demonstrates the value of audit in making baseline judgements about effectiveness. It also provides a useful basis for more systematic ABAB type study to compare outcomes of surgeons having "an interest in the field" with those who are specialists in the same field.

As has been alluded to earlier, data gathering for audit is time consuming. Given the variety of protocols and software packages in use, very little transferability or standardisation is possible. However Dunn et al (1994) reported a study demonstrating just how such problems can be minimised. The study demonstrated how clinicians' time can be put to more effective use in data gathering strategies as well as harnessing information technology. A mechanism was devised to access data on different software (PAS and the UNIX theatre management systems) thus enabling clinicians to access and input data in a meaningful way.

The exercise indicated the ease with which clinicians can come to terms with transferring data from one data base to personal computers and in creating custom made packages. They illustrated the "extent to which prospective data collection without audit assistants; can be a reliable source of clinical activity data". Likewise work by Barlow, Flynn and Britton in 1994 highlighted the extent to which computerised custom-made audit systems can be developed. Evidently, clinicians are becoming more aware of the value of audit in aiding clinical decision making. It is also obvious that a direct "hands on" can promote and sustain a research based culture.

In this context, a number of additional questions arise and include :-

- how does audit relate to the research culture of the NHS?
- what role can audit play in the quest for evidence based practice?
- how can audit be used as a mechanisms for promoting research ?

It is not the intention here to address all of these issues in detail. It is however essential to attempt an outline, as this will enrich the base upon which this study relies. This will be dealt with in Chapter 2.

Audit, as we have established earlier, can be seen as an essential process of review and monitoring, based on effective data gathering mechanisms. Clinicians and practitioners spend a good deal of time ensuring that data sets across a range of performance areas are collated so as to allow for the assessment of trends and patterns of care.

Williams proposes that "audit aims, where possible, to improve health care, and this can only happen when the audit includes some mechanism for change".

Williams does not specify what mechanisms constitute those that are intended to improve health care and leaves it open for clinicians to consider their particular approaches. He does however list a number of strategies/actions that have been used in the name of audit and then goes on to show what limitations they each have, as follows:-

Type of action	Examples
Data handling	data collection and information technology
Research	any empirical activity
Surgical epidemiology	activity analysis
Outcomes investigation	local validation study mortality and morbidity study comparative outcomes audit patient satisfaction surveys
clinical audit	development of an audit tool audit of other professionals audit of own health care

Each of these broad categories of information have been accounted for in terms of demonstrating how much they approximate to the full meaning of the concept/term. Williams suggests that the collection and manipulation of data, whilst being essential aspects of the audit process, are not in themselves audit.

An example cited included that of :-

> ## "a computerised data base and grading system for plastic surgery outcomes"

Our own data, for instance, catalogue information about diagnosis, characteristics of breast cancer and treatment approaches as cases in point. In context of data handling, Williams argues that data of this kind will yield nothing useful, unless specific questions are asked. He proposed for instance that data of the kind cited above could be used to address a number of questions and purposes including:-

measuring workload	activity analysis
informing managers and purchasers	operational research and planning
investigating the natural history of the disease	epidemiological research
investigating outcomes of treatment	research
providing information to clinicians about the quality of their treatment and of ways in which it could be improved	audit
an aid/information for teaching	education

In these examples, Williams is enunciating a variety of ways in which data gathering can be used to serve several stakeholders. In this sense, audit is but one way of gathering data. He indicates the cost and labour intensity of data collection and recommends the need to formulate questions at the outset of data collection as it is "common to find that important data have not been included... as data do not become information until specific questions are asked and answered" page 406. We concur on this point and will in effect trace how our data gathering strategy has forced us to consider a number of key questions that will be addressed in order to inform practice.

Williams makes a distinction between research and audit on the following basis. He asserts that "research seeks to discover new information"; whereas "audit seeks to improve health care". We would wish to question this difference, as it can be argued that research is much more than just the discovery of new information. In the positivistic tradition, research is primarily about falsification and verification. In this way research is about confirmation of what is the case. We firmly believe that audit allows the clinician to raise research questions and concur with Williams that this should be done at the outset. Research allows one to test hypotheses, but it is also possible to use audit data to perform similar tests if, and only if, hypotheses are formulated at the outset. This allows the data collection to be constructed in such a manner to make testing possible.

At this point it may be helpful to summarise the perceived differences and similarities between audit and research.

Audit	Research
emphasis on effecting change and technical improvements to the quality of care in order to meet pre defined local targets	focus on the process, not pre-stated expectations of the outcome of the work; results may be used to inform policy
is mainly reactive to local concerns or external requirements for scrutiny. however recent attempts by the British Breast Group and the BASO for instance have shown how nationally agreed guidelines could provide the basis of a national framework	can be proactive and be used to inform policy setting nationally
professionals set local targets appropriate to their respective knowledge and expectations	may involve wider peer group input into the research protocol or hypothesis
focus on participants who take part in audit as part of their operational roles	usually takes a substantial portion of the participants available time
medical audit is predominantly distinct from multi-disciplinary audit, quality control initiatives or general management	research is usually carried out by a third party
audit draws on national standards and guidance to inform local targets	research may be innovative and not be framed by any previous parameters or guidance
usually carried out for primarily local reasons; publication, dissemination and diffusion of results is secondary outside the local area. less likely to be set against national and international activity in comparative terms, although national and professional standards will be used to inform the local objectives	expectation that the work will be published widely and set in the context of comparative national and international research.

With regard to surgical epidemiology, Williams reflects on the spate of activity and "enormous efforts" dedicated to information gathering about surgical treatment. He suggests that unless such information gathering is associated with standard setting and that comparisons of the quality of care against agreed standards are made, then such activity should not be described as audit. More importantly, he argues that mechanisms to accommodate changes arising out of such comparisons should also be in place. He cites the following example of an activity analysis :-

"a retrospective analysis was carried out of activity over 5 years, including types of surgery, deaths, complications and status of operator".

Williams identified the key objective of the above exercise as an attempt to demonstrate "that valuable experience in paediatric surgery was possible for trainees in a district general hospital, and that the complication rate was low". He asserts that with such an objective, the focus of the study was more in the lap of operational research than that of an audit study as there was no mechanism for bringing about any changes or improvement to care. Whilst this may be the case , it can be argued that the analysis may have yielded findings which may point to the cost effectiveness of the particular strategy. As such this could provide vital information for the planning and resourcing of the service that the clinical director and manager may find of immense value.

Williams attempts to explain the differences associated with outcomes investigations, whether they take the form of a local validation study or morbidity and mortality study, as suffering from problems of not incorporating standard settings in the first place. Moreover, they allow little or no scope for changing practice. Patient satisfaction surveys suffer in a similar way. It is evident that data derived from such studies may be instrumental in allowing standards to be defined and set in an audit study. It has to be conceded though that most satisfaction survey studies begin with an orientation which is focused on gathering information about consumer or patient satisfaction. In these circumstances it is difficult to justify them as audits per se. In some cases personnel are inclined to confuse the use of the terms "consumer audit" and "patient satisfaction surveys" as they are used interchangeably, in health care settings.

The health care reforms, and in particular the NHS & Community Care Act 1990 have brought about substantial changes which warrant more attention to developing mechanisms for using audit in health care services. Such intentions have been supported by financial incentives and funding manifest in the appointment of mainly non-clinical staff to advise and execute audits across the spectrum. This strategy would on face value seem to afford vital support to clinicians who can make use of it in using audit in a more constructive and efficient way. More importantly they are able to direct attention to selected areas for audit, agree standards, discuss the evidence derived and take a lead in implementing the change in practice.

Williams asserts that audit as a process requires the use of an "audit tool" which in essence is a method of collecting or analysing data when the information obtained is to be used to improve health care. Tools used could include a wide array of instruments including:-

- data collection spreadsheet
- questionnaire
- computerised data base

Whatever strategy is adopted, the uses to which such instruments could be put are many and varied. Clinicians may be inclined to audit the work of their own practice or that of the work of others. The present culture based on emergent concerns for evidence and value for money makes it more imperative that clinicians use their time effectively and appropriately. To assert or establish a case without verifiable evidence is no longer sustainable. Against this background is the realisation, as Williams noted that many clinicians "despise audit as a waste of their time, and regard it as poor substitute for research". He accounted for this in the sense that they have received little support or assistance or simply do not fully understand its " objectives and methods".

A similar sentiment was echoed by Devlin (1996) who argued that "clinical audit should lead to an improvement in care; for a surgeon, this means ensuring that effective evidence based surgical management be provided to all our patients". He went on to spell out the role that the Royal College of Surgeons aims to fulfil in promoting education and training on audit.

The origins of audit in the NHS
Audit now has a well established history in the National Health service. It has been developed in a methodical and now rigorous system from its early origins in the Korner data sets of the 1970's. It has progressed to a more systematic record in the form of Performance Indicators and more recently into Health Service Statistics. Indeed the recent emphasis attached to the publication of league tables in respect of Patient Charter Initiatives, Health of the Nation

targets or even regionally based figures of hospital and surgeons workload indicate the burgeoning use of audit figures.

Audit has a central role to serve in breast cancer. This sentiment has been strongly echoed by a number of reports and policy directives. For instance, the British Breast Group recommends that the "collection of data on outcomes" is vital in order to monitor and review treatment and management of the condition. Specifically, the BBG recommends that specialist Breast units should:-

"carry out regular audit of the process and outcome of care."

In addition, the Report of the Working party of the British Breast Group (July 1994) made explicit that staff working in specialist breast units "should participate in external quality assurance schemes". The working party noted the important role that data gathering can play in monitoring and reviewing of services. In this regard they go on to suggest that such auditing of breast cancer care should form a part of the contracting services. They further recommended that "all breast units should keep accurate and computerised data sets of diagnostic, staging, treatment and follow up data". They perceived the valuable role that such data can serve in assessing the outcomes of care.

The Clinical Outcomes Group Subgroup proposals for the characteristics likely to be associated with good outcomes enumerated 11 aspects of a comprehensive service for breast cancer management. These include:-

- patient centred care, information for patients and psycho-social support
- diagnostic facilities and procedures
- surgery
- radiotherapy
- systemic therapies, including hormone manipulation and chemotherapy
- palliative care
- the specialist breast care team
- effective inter-professional communication
- clinical guidelines, up-to-date practice and continuing medical education
- environment and facilities

At first glance it is obvious that all of these aspects can be seen as essential parameters for audit. Indeed, it is possible that several breast cancer units are attempting to evaluate the data gathered on these indicators.

The NHSE has devised a number of mechanisms for addressing effectiveness and efficiency within the health service. One of the primary mechanisms is that of enhancing education and awareness. The NHSE publication on "Promoting Clinical Effectiveness", for instance, demonstrates a strategy and series of action points that can be taken to strengthen the link between research based knowledge and routine clinical practice.

A mechanism for sustaining the link is that of the recently established structure in which the NHSE works through professional bodies through the Clinical Outcomes Group (COG). The aims of COG are primarily to improve ways in which clinical guidelines are developed and used in the NHS. This is required because there is obvious recognition and appreciation of the value of good quality guidelines which are based on evidence of effectiveness. This can be schematised as follows:-

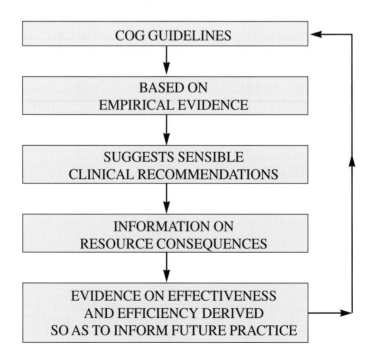

Alan Langlands, Chief Executive of the National Health Service Executive firmly believes that adequate "good quality" information currently exists and that this should be used to support local strategies to promote clinical effectiveness. Of specific relevance here is the recommendation that local strategies ought to be able to;-

"use clinical outcomes and clinical audit to influence changes in the service"

"to identify the source and use of information to judge the effectiveness of services"

"to demonstrate the manner in which patients are being informed about effectiveness related to their treatment"

It is suggested that it is through these series of actions that providers can work in partnership with purchasers to ensure that appropriate investment is made in effective intervention which matches the health care needs of the locality.

In summary then, we have attempted to discuss a range of issues pertaining to the principles and practice of audit. We wish to assert that these issues provide a common base of knowledge and understanding on audit. Clinicians and practitioners across specialities would be able to draw upon this and apply it as their circumstances require.

With regards to breast cancer, it is evident that a number of protocols and formats on breast cancer care auditing exist and include for instance :-

A Breast Cancer Audit Strategy for South Thames designed by the Health Care Evaluation Unit at St Georges Medical School: London

The North Thames Prospective Audit of Present Cancer Management: Information Pack for providers produced by the Thames Cancer Registry

The Breast Unit Database: Version 1.0 produced by the British Association of Surgical Oncologists.

As we have noted, Williams has indicated the negative perception that some clinicians harboured of audit. Others regard it as a poor substitute for research. We suggest that this may be related to the fact that they have never received appropriate support or assistance to carry out audit. It is further possible that they neither understand its objectives and methods, nor appreciate its potential for improving health care.

In addition, most Breast Cancer Units would have developed their own data sets as they assess and design their case load. In Chapter 3 we will revisit these in order to discuss the rationale for choosing particular items in the construction of a breast cancer audit protocol. For now though, we wish to consider the relationship between audit and research and to assess the extent to which audit can provide a useful function in the emergence of evidence based practice.

Chapter 2

In this chapter we aim to:-

- discuss audit in the context of an emerging research based culture in the NHS

- outline the role of audit in supporting the development of evidence based practice

- demonstrate the role of audit in the facilitation of action based research

- demonstrate that the questions on which we are focusing in our breast cancer audit are part and parcel of reflection in practice.

Audit in context of an emerging research based culture in the NHS

This audit study of breast cancer care has core principles which are of value to any other audit study. We propose to identify these within a wider framework to demonstrate the value to clinicians and practitioners in other fields. We have previously discussed the theoretical basis of audit and of its role in supporting a research based culture. Our approach will be comprehensive and will use our study to illustrate experiences and practice.

In the first chapter, we made clear that whilst we agreed with the broad thrust of the arguments proposed by Williams (1996), we would wish to argue that audit is a useful basis for supporting and developing empirical activity. We will suggest that the questions asked at the outset of an audit study do not differ from those asked in a research study. The testing of hypotheses require questions to be posed at the outset. Data gathered in an audit study can enable those hypotheses to be tested. Of course, audits will vary from those that require ABAB type designs, commonly used in experimental studies, or those used in clinical trials and evaluation studies. We see audit studies as designs on a continuum which are of value in research oriented cultures. Given this line of reasoning, how can audit be strengthened in context of the NHS? To answer this question we will need to examine recent attempts at promoting research within the NHS.

Research has recently attracted substantial attention in the treatment and delivery of health care. Since the NHS and Community Care Act 1990, a number of policy directives have emanated from the National Health Service Executive, that have impacted upon strategic and operational outcomes of research. That the NHS is taking research seriously is manifest by the centrality of the organisational structure, now established at senior level to direct and shape research policy. This structure takes the form of the Research and Development Directorate which is headed by a Director of R&D (DRD). This role is afforded strategic importance and the DRD is a member of the NHS Executive Board.

The DRD is supported by an NHS Executive Branch of the Department of Research and Development Division (RDD). This division works in an integrated fashion across the three business branches of the Department and is instrumental in shaping and determining the nature of research work across other divisions. The R&D Directorate is further supported at NHS level through the regional network of Regional Drectors and Regional Offices.

The R&D strategy has been based upon wide and detailed consultation. The strategy continues to be refined beginning with the publication of the NHS R&D strategy in April 1991, followed by the strategic statement Research & Health in Sept 1992. These policies were futher extended by the Research and Health publication in June 1993. Subsequently, co-ordination of the R&D strategy was modified as a result of the publication of "Managing the New NHS; Function and Responsibility" in July 1994. This paper outlined how R&D would be managed by the NHS. It further explained the role of the NHSE and of the Regional Offices.

Recently, the work of the Independent Task Force led by Professor Anthony Culyer provided the basis for a strategy to support and develop Research in the NHS into the next century. That report, "Supporting Research and Development in the NHS" (EL 94/68), maps out the framework for developing a partnership approach between the NHS and other stakeholders including the Universities, Research Councils, Voluntary Organisations and Charities.

What then are the key objectives of the R&D strategy?

The basis of the strategy centres around six main objectives which are as follows:-

(a) *Identifying NHS requirements for research and science based knowledge*

(b) *Ensuring that knowledge relevant to the NHS requirements is forthcoming*

(c) *Ensuring that information about research based knowledge is available to decision makers*

(d) *Promoting the use of R&D findings*

(e) *Promoting an evaluation culture*

(f) *Developing and evaluating the R&D strategy*

Whilst it is evident that a great deal of consideration has been instilled in the development of the R&D strategy, questions remain about the impact it has made on the clinician at service level. These pertain to the extent to which clinicians are encouraged to undertake and participate in research. Furthermore, there is the major issue of the extent to which clinicians act upon research questions. There are however a number of related issues that may help to cement the effects that Evidence Based Medicine promote. In effect, the R&D strategy is but one of a number of inter-related actions which may impact upon practitioners in promoting EBM.

To summarise then, research within the health service is now centrally driven and has absorbed a good deal of attention and resourcing towards the development of an infra-structure for promoting and instigating research. This infra-structure is illustrated in Diagrams 4, 5 and 6.

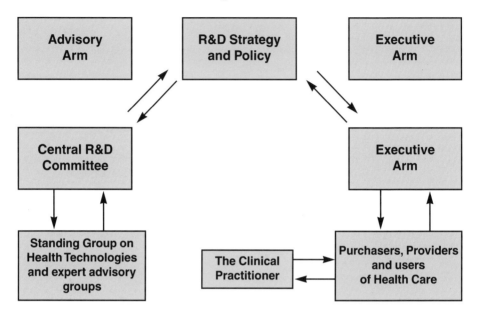

Fig 4.　**NHS R&D Structure and Function**

NHS Management Executive

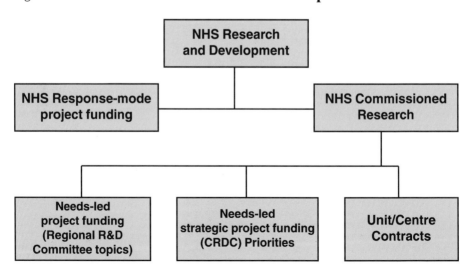

Fig 5.　**NHS Research and Development**

Fig 6.

R&D Input to Purchasing

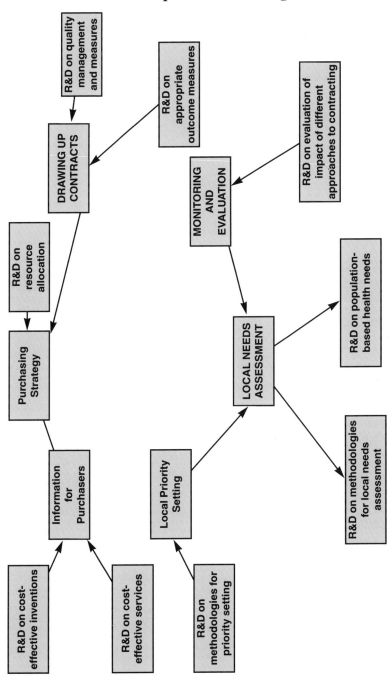

We will later outline the action that can be taken by clinicians to make use of the research infra-structure. Now, we wish to pursue four other issues that impinge upon the development of a research based culture in the NHS, and these are as follows:-

- The NHS and Community Care Act stipulation on research

- The Calman Working Group Report on professionally based clinical education

- The role of reflection in practice as a basis of developing clinical practice

- The emergence of evidence based practice

The NHS and Community Care Act stipulation on research

The NHS & Community Care Act (1990) makes explicit commitment to the role of Hospital Trusts in respect of research under Section 2: para (11) as follows:-

"An NHS Trust may undertake and commission research and make available staff and provide facilities for research by other persons" (page 80). The Act, whilst recognising a role for the Trust in respect of engaging in and allowing for the conduct of research does not make this an obligation as such. It evidently falls on individual clinicians and practitioners, to pursue such activity as part and parcel of their work in their respective roles in providing clinical services. Clinical staff have the advantage of attracting substantial funding and support from medical research councils, medical charities as well as the pharmaceutical industry.

As the role of hospital trusts emerge within what is becoming an ever increasing competitive market, the organisation and development of research at institutional level, may become more systematised. This will harness, multi-professional research in the same way as multi-professional audit.

The Calman enquiry on professionally based clinical education

That audit is important for the development of professional competence has taken on additional emphasis, given the Secretary of State Working group chaired by Sir Kenneth Calman, which resulted in the publication of the "Hospital Doctors; Training for the future"; the report of the Working Group on Specialist Medical Training. The group was established in 1993 to identify action necessary to harmonise U.K medical training in line with E.C directives. The underlying concern was for action on mutual recognition of specialist medical training in the E.U in respect of E.C 1975 directives. The Working Group's terms of reference were to focus primarily on "a consideration of the present U.K arrangements for post-graduate medical education on career progression in the NHS, taking into account E.C law" (page 1).

The DoH Working Group on Specialist Medical Training (1992) led to the publication of "Hospital doctors: Training for the future". This was followed up by the publication of " A guide to the Specialist Registrar Training", in March 1996.

This report argued that "changes will produce shorter, more structured and organised training" so that independent clinical competence as a consultant can be achieved earlier, than has been the case before. The report indicated that NHS Trusts and Health Authorities have a role to play in specialist registrar training placements by working in partnership with post graduate deans and in providing the environment in which training can take place successfully.

The Annexe of the Specialist Registrar Training Programme specifies, amongst a range of requirements, that the Clinician "understands the principles of audit and to show evidence of participation in the same". Additionally, a desirable quality is that the respondent (in this case the clinician) understands the principles and demonstrates evidence of enthusiasm or participation in research.

Section 17 of the Guide to Specialist Registrar Training asserts that "there is a requirement for all doctors to have an understanding of the scientific method, an appreciation of research methodologies and the capacity to assess critically a contribution to research".

Whilst it is not the intention here to discuss fully the basis of the consultation process and other deliberations of the Working Group, it is nonetheless necessary to consider elements of the focus on training which the Royal Colleges and Faculties have developed. The Working Group acknowledges the guiding principles which should inform specialist medical training as follows:

"that specialist training is an integral part of a wider continuum of medical education and training which begins on entry to medical school and is only completed on retirement from active practice"

"that any changes proposed must ensure that standards of both medical training and clinical services to patients are maintained or improved"

"that the assessment of doctors would be based on competence".

In respect of the training length, structure and content of the curriculum leading to the Certificate of Completion of Specialist Training (CCST), the working group consulted widely and recorded advice in which the "majority commented on the need for training to be structured....most envisaged a more flexible system with some specifying that learning objectives should be set for the individual". There was some emphasis on the need for training to cover "non-clinical skills, such as management, audit and communication".

Concern was also expressed that a more intensive training period might lessen the opportunity for research. A small number of respondents suggested that research should be retained as an option for training. The Working Group commissioned a number of sub-groups to assist with its enquiry. The sub-group commissioned to enquire into the current and proposed training programme, with particular reference to structure and duration considered a range of issues. These included the nature and length of specialist training, entry requirement, assessment, impediments to effective training, as well as on the issue of research.

The subgroup recommended that "further consideration be given to the role and opportunities for research during specialist training and in particular, requirements of doctors pursuing a career in academic medicine".

The Royal College of Surgeons proposed arrangements indicating that in respect of higher professional training, a number of strategies can be used including:-

- entry requirements in course log books
- annual assessments through course reports, log books
- opportunities for a period of research

As these frameworks are being devised two key questions can be posed as follows:-

- what role can audit play in the quest for evidence based practice?
- how can audit be used as a mechanism for promoting research?

The role of auditing in the new health service with respect to EVIDENCE BASED MEDICINE

The health care reforms manifest in the NHS & Community Care Act (1990) have been predicated upon a number of major concerns for what are now commonly regarded as the three "E"s viz.: Effectiveness, Efficiency and Economy. That such concerns are paramount can be noted in a continuous train of policy directives emanating from the National Health Service Executive. Most recently this ideology has been explicitly re-stated by Alan Langlands, Chief Executive of the NHSE, who asserted that:-

> "the purpose of the NHS is to secure through the resources available, the greatest possible improvement to the health of the people of England. In order to achieve this, we must continue to improve the clinical and cost effectiveness of services throughout the NHS by formulating decisions on the basis of appropriate evidence about clinical effectiveness. This is one of the medium term priorities in the NHS priorities and Planning Guidance (PPG) for 1996/97".
>
> para 1. EL (95) 105

The drive towards effectiveness, efficiency and economy has been substantially supported by an infrastructure for developing evidence based practice. It is not the intention of this report to devote substantial attention to the history and value of evidence based practice as this has been well addressed elsewhere. (See, for instance, Sackett 1979). It is however, essential to address the issue in passing as it plays a pivotal role in the formation of an effective service and in this specific context provides an agenda for developing an effective breast cancer service.

Summary of the EBM movement.

Long and Harrison (1995) in a series of short briefing papers in the Health Service Journal; Health Management Guide, provided an account of evidence based medicine. They asserted that it "reflects the aspiration that doctors and other clinical professionals should pursue their work of diagnosis, therapy and care on the basis of procedures which are known through research evidence, to be effective". Given the potential for health care, it is not surprising that there are now wide-spread attempts to make this approach the core issue in the health services, by promoting what is regarded as evidence based practice.

Rosenberg and Donald (1995) defined EBM as "the process of systematically investigating, appraising, and using contemporaneous research findings as the basis for clinical decisions". Here, four distinct but overlapping phases can be identified:-

- formulation of clear clinical questions from patients' or organisational problems
- conducting a literature search for relevant clinical articles

The range and quality of papers here may be of variable quality and using a variety of methodologies. The clinician will need to exercise systematic critical appraisal using set criteria to make judgements of worth on the papers selected. In some cases, meta-review papers may be available on the topic under consideration and in these circumstances critical appraisal would have already been undertaken as such.

- evaluating or carrying out a critical appraisal of the evidence so as to derive an account of its validity and relevance
- act upon, through implementation of the findings

The Cochrane Centre defines evidence based medicine (practice) as the process of life long, self directed learning, in which clinicians (and practitioners):-

- *convert their clinical information needs into answerable questions*
- *track down the best evidence with which to answer these questions*

- *critically appraise the evidence for its validity and usefulness*
- *apply the results of that appraisal to the care of their patients*
- *evaluate their performance*

We welcome the importance attached to the value of "life long and self directed learning". Indeed, as the work of Houle (1981) and others remind us, these values constitute the defining qualities and hall mark of established professions. Life long and self directed learning are key attributes in the making of professionals.

Houle identified 14 characteristics associated with the professionalisation process. These can be grouped into two categories, one conceptual and the other, regarded as the collective identity characteristics. In the first set, Houle described five key aspects as follows:-

1. members of the profession should be concerned with clarifying its defining function
2. mastery of theoretical knowledge
3. capacity to solve problems
4. use of practical knowledge
5. self enhancement

The other category consists the remaining characteristics which include:-

6. formal training
7. credentialling ie testing the capacity of practitioners to perform at a competent level
8. creation of a sub culture
9. legal reinforcement
10. public acceptance
11. ethical practice
12. penalties
13. relationships with other vocations
14. relations to users of services.

Evidently, a number of these characteristics reinforce the need for theoretical, empirical as well as practice based reflections.

That the medical profession is now so committed to the cause and practice of EBM is witnessed by the recent establishment of the Centre for Evidence Based Medicine located in Oxford University's Nuffield Department of Clinical Medicine at the John Radcliffe hospital. The Centre's objectives are threefold as follows:-

- *its intention to promote the teaching, learning, practice and evaluation of evidence based medicine and evidence based health care throughout the UK*

This clearly requires a partnership approach in which the R&D strategy is reinforced by an expectation from the Royal Colleges that clinicians will demonstrate evidence of continuing education, in order to satisfy conditions for periodic re-registration. Furthermore, the recent obligations outlined in the Calman report regarding requirements for learning in the clinical environment, point to an infrastructure supporting the drive towards enquiry, research and effectiveness in health care service delivery. As a consequence it is evident that practice based developments and quality of care can be enhanced by a range of activities. Audit, as one element of this approach provides an effective and useful strategy.

- *to devise a strategy and action plan to conduct applied, patient based and methodological research in order to generate the new knowledge required for the practice of evidence based health care*
- *to collaborate with other scientists in the creation of a graduate programme to train researchers to perform randomised controlled trials and systematic reviews*

We recognise the fundamental role that evidence based practice has in stimulating a research based culture. However, we are aware of some of the problems associated with a reliance on evidence based strategies on their own.

Reflection on practice.

The concept of "reflection on practice" is not new, specially with regard to vocational education in the caring professions. Indeed in some professions such as teaching and nursing, there exists a substantial body of knowledge attesting to the increasing importance that is attached to the development and use of reflection on practice. It is essential to explore the concept and to trace its historical roots in the development of its use in professional practice.

A number of well established accounts can be considered here. Boyd & Fales (1983) have argued that "reflective learning is the process of internally examining an issue of concern, triggered by an experience, which creates and clarifies meaning in terms of self and which results in changed conceptual perspective". Boud (1985) claims that "reflection in context of learning is a generic term for those intellectual and affective activities in which individuals engage to explore their experiences in order to lead to a new understanding and experience". Here it is obvious that reflection embodies both intellectual and affective activities which may impact upon the development of professionally focused knowledge. Like many other theorists on this subject, Boud does not offer a typology of "intellectual and affective" activities embodied in reflective practice.

One of the foremost contributions to our understanding of reflection on practice has been derived from the work of Schon (1987) who regards reflection as having two distinct elements. On the one hand there is a focus on reflection in action and by this Schon means thinking on one's feet. The other element refers to a stimulus to abstract thought. It is through the combination of these two inter-dependent activities that Schon believes that insight and knowledge can be derived from practice. These ideas are schematised in the model proposed by Schon as follows:-

The theoretical basis of experiential learning.

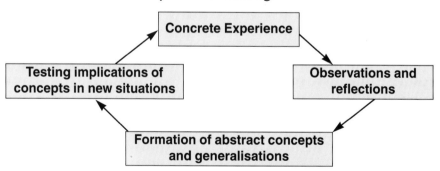

Schon is attempting to promote an idea that through reflection on the practice, one can derive a body of intuitive learning and knowledge. This, when used effectively can enhance understanding of the nature of one's work. Schon's model also implies that reflection as an attribute could stimulate abstract and other problem solving qualities. We believe that this is the basis which audit and research can benefit from. It is the model which underpins our audit on breast cancer care.

A map of practice, reflection, audit and research

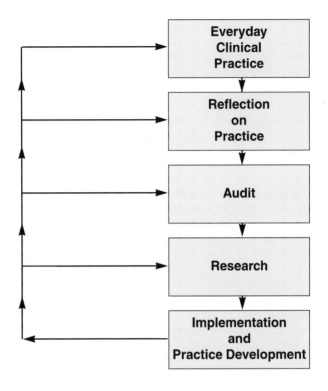

Our model does not rigidly imply that in the real world of clinical practice and medical research, each of the stages identified are distinct. Indeed it could be argued that there are considerable overlaps and influences affecting the respective stages. One needs to concede that the scientific enterprise, with its reliance on the hypothetico-deductive approach, still poses a number of serious philosophical problems as there remain questions about the value of the role of falsification and verification in the generation of research based knowledge. The Popperian view of falsification is not as clear cut as earlier defined. Furthermore, Baum & Colletta (1995) and Baum (1996) have suggested, based on an analysis of existing research, and for that matter, on the plethora of treatment approaches used, that further work is still necessary to establish a dominant research paradigm on the treatment of breast cancer. Our argument is that through reflection on practice, audit and rigorous empirical studies, clinicians, researchers and scientists would arrive at "new and better ideas" on the treatment and management of the condition.

Chapter 3

In this chapter we wish to address the following issues:-

- the formulation of questions for the audit data
- the conduct of the audit
- methodology

From our past experience and through the process of refining our work, we have identified a number of questions that we wanted to ask. Initially some of these were not framed with research in mind although we had intuitively felt that the information might prove important. Some of the questions are consistent with recommendations made by specialist working groups as we will discuss later. Others were posed as they have potential value in planning and managing the breast service. We also intend to examine findings which provide a base for empirical comparisons, at a time when a great deal of research work is unfolding in the field.

Initial questions arising from the concerns we had were:-

- what are the real mortality figures in these cohorts?
- what are the real recurrence figures?
- what is the mean time to death?
- what is the mean time to recurrence?
- what is the effect of age?

These questions began to exercise our minds in terms of :-

- what data should we gather?
- what items should we begin with?
- what other issues can we examine in respect of the two cohorts (i.e. the Screen Detected or Symptomatic)

Early thoughts concerning the two cohorts provided a range of questions on:-

- Volume of patients seen within a time frame:comparisons with national trends
- Age cohorts of women

- Consultation times/diagnosis times
- Types of conditions
- Size of tumours
- Grade of tumours
- Types of tumours and side of body affected
- Type of tumour and treatment
- Treatment and recurrence free period
- Type of tumour and mortality figures

At this point we wish to indicate the range of data sets recommended by other agencies in comparison with our own:-

MDS :Cancer Registries: EL (92) 95	BASO (data sets on software)	Garvigan (data sets recommended)	Worthing (data sets on spread sheet used)
Name	Name address, postcode	Timescale: referral to treatment	(All demographic data, history and investigation details accessed via hospital number and case notes) Hospital No.
Address	Referral and attendance	No. of pt visits prior to diagnosis	Age diagnosis date
Postcode	Past history clinical presentation; clinical findings	Proportion of pre-op diagnosis for palpable lesions	
Sex	Investigations	No. of therapeutic operations	Last seen date
DOB	Radiology mammography; breast ultrasound; overall radiological opinion	Pathological size and grade of lesion	Survival
Previous surname	Pathology cytology; histology and codes side affected; grade; diagnosis	Proportion of invasive cancer with known nodal status	Ductal

Marital Status	Location and classification of malignancy	Proportion of cases where diagnosis and treatment plan discussed at multi-disciplinary meeting	Lobular
NHS no.	Communication of diagnosis & treatment planning	Proportion of cases where a breast care nurse is available to see pt pre & post op	Tubular
Date of death	Treatment: surgery	Pt involvement in choice of treatment	DCIS/LCIS/rare
Disease specific	Treatment: adjuvant therapies	Radiotherapy -offered -given -timescale	Size (mm)
Site of primary growth Side	Treatment: chemotherapy	Endocrine therapy Chemotherapy -offered -given -time scale	Grade/nodes positive Treatment: DXT/CMX/Tam
Type and behaviour of growth		Proportion of cases where trial eligibility and entry are established	Affected side
Record, type and registration details		Outcome measures repeat surgery complications	Mastectomy second operation.
Multiple tumour and death; certificate only indicators		Lymphoedema local recurrence regional recurrence contra lateral 1. breast cancers metastases death	

Basis of diagnosis		Process Measurement ease of referral/ interface with primary care	Residual tumour
Treatment		Psychological support and supply of relevant information	Vascular invasion.
Stage and grade of tumour		Radiotherapy fractionation policies	Interval to 1st recurrence.
Screening data option at present as are occupation and ethnicity.		Prostheses service	Death date
		Palliative care 90% of FNA samples adequate appropriate treatment for DCIS Outcome indicators Morbidity (QoL) Mortality Satisfaction	Interval to death cause code of death entry to trials comments

Methodology

The study is based on a retrospective audit using existing arrangements for data gathering within the unit. This is made possible as the West Sussex Breast Centre has for the past three years employed a Clinical Trials Co-ordinator. The key roles of this post holder include:-

- Entering suitable patients into trials.
- Maintaining the data base
- Extracting required information from the data base

The Clinical Trials Co-ordinator fulfils a key role in data gathering and at this point it is worthwhile to give an account of the manner in which the data set was devised and collected.

In August 1989, when the West Sussex Breast Screening Programme started, one of us in the role of surgeon, began to collect data prospectively. Screen detected cases requiring operations were entered into a special register in theatre. Benign or malignant pathology was identified. The type of operation was noted including localisation by ultrasound or needle. Symptomatic cases were entered onto a card system in a similar manner. This process was the sole responsibility of the surgeon, until the arrival of the clinical trials co-ordinator (CTC). It was during this period that the symptomatic breast service at Worthing was being reorganised to run on the same basis as that for screening, using the same multidisciplinary team. A fast track mammographic follow up clinic was also established.

Prior to this, Worthing was dealing with over 200 breast cancers every year. There was a notion that the true mortality was lower than the national figures suggested. In addition, it seemed that the mean time to recurrence and death from breast cancer was longer than estimated. Tumour behaviour also seemed to be variable and this was evident particularly in our elderly patients. It seemed that there was now an opportunity to examine these questions and gather data which could be analysed to inform our practice.

With the arrival of the CTC, addressing these issues became possible. The first task was to include, retrospectively, all symptomatic cancers going back to August 1989, using the card system. Here, it should be noted that computerisation within the hospital was in its infancy and there was a culture change to be made. There were, however, questions being asked and data available to answer them. A data base was devised, first on paper, and then transferred to a spreadsheet. It had to be easy to manage and update. The data sets had to be decided in advance and it was accepted that there would be some information that might be required at a later date. A decision was taken, early on, to include all private patients. All available data were then entered onto the spreadsheet leaving only screen detected cases to be collected as before. This was to act as a safety valve to ensure accuracy.

For the purpose of this study and future comparison, patients are divided into two groups consisting of Cohort 1 and Cohort 2:-

Cohort 1
This group will, hereafter, be referred to as the symptomatic group. This includes all patients attending the breast clinic at Worthing Hospital who have

been referred by their General Practitioner. No attempt has been made to assess the time between presentation to GP and appointment to the clinic. All patients had visited their GP with concerns about their breasts prior to referral.

Cohort 2

This group will, hereafter, be referred to as Breast Screening Unit (BSU) group. These patients have had mammography as part of the National Breast Screening Programme and are generally symptom free 'well' women.

Decision making about the data set to be recorded

As has been discussed earlier, the nature and amount of data that should be recorded in a breast cancer audit is still a matter for debate. The recently devised protocol by the health care evaluation unit at St.Georges Hospital has not been met with approval from the specialists' units. Most units have attempted to modify the recommendations by the BBG and BASO into a workable model based upon their local practices. Certain features of our data sets are self selecting, based upon outcomes in diagnosis and treatment as follows:-

a) Firstly, confirmation of breast cancer diagnosis usually follows either a fine needle aspiration (FNA), wide bore needle histology or surgical biopsy. This provides the first data set and becomes the 'diagnosis date'.

b) Data about the symptomatic cohort were stored on cards and in some cases there were gaps.

c) Data on the Breast Screening cohort are stored in theatre books and here there are no gaps.

An administrative procedure had been routinely set-up for all breast clinic notes to be returned to Clinical Trials Co-ordinator after breast and general surgery clinics. The CTC trawls the notes prior to breast/general surgery clinics and attaches a label to the notes requesting their return to the CTC. Medical Secretaries are also requested to direct any such case notes to the CTC before returning to file.

Stage 1

This procedure then allows for what is regarded as Stage 1 data gathering. Here emphasis is placed on completion of the missing gaps in tumour statistics of both the Symptomatic and Breast Screening cohorts by a series of actions including:

- checking notes after the clinics
- selecting notes and checking pathology forms
- trawling the breast/general surgery clinic notes and labelling for return to co-ordinator's office after clinics
- the notes of patients with complete entries are marked (year of diagnosis on the return label which remains in-situ on all breast patient notes) and returned to file.

Stage 2 data gathering procedures include the following actions:-

- to seek out any patients not accounted for on 'cards'
- request made to the regional breast screening office for a print out of all symptomatic patients (BSU patient data complete) registered from 1991 to present
- this list of 700 patients cross checked and any patients already known about crossed off
- the remaining patients were divided into two categories (1) seen by surgeons in breast centre and (2) seen privately
- requests made to regional screening office for pathology on all screened patients
- over a period of 3 months all notes were examined (including a small number of private patients)
- demographic details and tumour statistics recorded
- patients who did not have surgery and therefore had no pathology form available tracked down from existing records and through breast clinics. It is accepted that this group of patients contains most gaps as many are domiciled in nursing homes with follow-up dealt by GPs.

Stage 3 data gathering procedures include the following actions:-

- Spreadsheet devised using Microsoft Excel Version 5.0 Spreadsheet package using purposeful and manageable criteria

- Data entered for two groups (1) symptomatic (2) screen detected to enable comparison and analysis.

The above actions and systems yielded data which were finally compiled under the following headings.

Spreadsheet Headings

Hosp No - for ease of updating records, reference mechanism, checking outcomes.

Age - at date of diagnosis.

Diagnosis date - date cancer confirmed either by Fine Needle Aspiration or histology.

Last seen - date last seen by any consultant and confirmed as recurrence free.

Survival - interval in months since diagnosis.

Tumour categories (eg:ductal - rare etc) - based on predominant tumour at time of diagnosis.

Tumour size (in mms) in the case of two or more tumours in same breast the largest tumour is recorded. Multifocal tumours are identified in the free text.

Grade - as reported on histology.

Nodes positive - number found positive irrespective of number removed. 0 indicates negative nodes after axillary surgery. **Blank** indicates no axillary surgery .

DXT (radiotherapy)   1 = yes   **Blank** = no

CMX (chemotherapy) 1 = yes   **Blank** = no

TAM (Tamoxifen)   1 = yes   **Blank** = no

Affected Side - **L** = left **R** = right.

Mast (mastectomy)   1 = yes   **Blank** = smaller operation or no surgery

As second op   1 = yes, mastectomy or further surgery such as wider excision or axillary staging.

Residual Tumour - residual tumour was found in the second specimen

Vasc Invas - vascular invasion found in specimen - used as an indicator of local recurrence.

Int to 1st rec (Interval to first recurrence) - interval in months from diagnosis date to first recurrence.

Date of Death - notified date of death.

Int to death (interval to death) - interval in months from diagnosis to death.

ER - Oestrogen receptor status.

Cause code - 1 = Breast Cancer: **2** = Not breast cancer **9** = unknown (but probably breast cancer)

Comments - free text:entry into randomised controlled trials recorded here

Entries thus agreed are then entered by the CTC and the consultant surgeons. Ongoing updates are achieved via breast clinics/GPs/death registrations. Progress of elderly or none attending patients (moved, deceased, too elderly, unwell etc) checked as far as possible through GPs and Hospital Information System. The final spread sheet data allows for statistical analysis which is the focus of Chapter 4.

Chapter 4.

In this chapter we provide a detailed analysis of our findings and raise a number of questions that will provide the basis of ongoing study. Furthermore, we will refer to research which informs the audit. In this way, we will demonstrate how audit can be used to instigate and inform on-going empirical work.

Data Analysis
The data sets determined as essential indicators were collated as a matter of routine. These details were entered on an ™Excel spread sheet by the Clinical Trials Co-ordinator (LT). These data sets were later assimilated on to a final spread sheet which is then checked by two of us (AS & LT). As part of the routine operations of the West Sussex Breast Centre, we then scrutinise the spread sheets to ascertain accuracy and update them on a weekly basis.

From this base line a hard copy of the ®Excel spreadsheet was coded and entered on SPSS. The data were then analysed by one of us (AK). The findings derived from this were then used to compile the results section of this publication.

Analysis conducted was treated to both descriptive and inferential statistical techniques. The range of tests were chosen based on questions posed at the outset.

Initial considerations
Two questions which arise are:-

- What inferences can be made about the volume of the patients seen in the two cohorts?
- How do these cohorts differ?

In order to address these, we will consider the issue of demography in the context of both local and regional populations. To recap, Cohort 1 is based on symptomatic patients, identified through general practitioner referrals. Cohort 2 refers to screen detected patients.

Number Of Patients In The Two Cohorts
Cohort 1 consists of 819 patients and Cohort 2 of 612 patients.

Fig 7: Size of cohorts

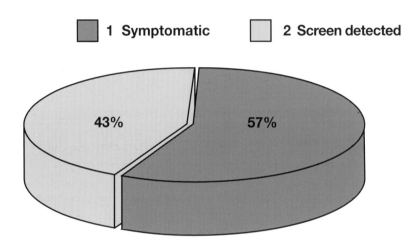

At face value the two groups differ in terms of volume. When treated to inferential tests (One way ANOVA) the figures represented in the volume of patients do not differ significantly (F= 1.858; P=173). We need to ask why there are more symptomatic patients seen at the Unit.

Breast screening started in West Sussex, based at Worthing Hospital in 1989. This focused on women between the ages of 50 and 64 years. All data on cancers detected were collected prospectively from the start. This Cohort of patients is well defined and results in about one hundred cancers detected over a twelve month period. This figure is unlikely to change though it may fall in the future.

It seemed logical that the same multi-disciplinary approach should be applied to symptomatic women i.e. those referred to the centre by their General Practitioner (GP). Over two years the service was reorganised so that all symptomatic patients were assessed in the same way. Any cancers detected as a result had the data collected prospectively. In the initial years symptomatic cancers were fewer. Since then numbers have increased and are in excess of the screen detected cancers. The reason for this is due to the time taken to redirect symptomatic patients as well as having collected retrospective data on all symptomatic cancers from the beginning of screening. As expected, since this is a much wider age range and since all patients now enter the system, the numbers are larger. Statistically these figures compare favourably, given the female population of the geographical catchment area.

BASO (1996) quoted DoH (1995) figures showing the average GP should expect to see 0.86 patients with a diagnosis of breast cancer every year. Our own analysis of yearly figures indicates a progressive increase year on year from 1990-1995. In 1996 the figures for both cohorts decreased. This may well reflect the expected reduction mentioned earlier.

Nonetheless, these figures indicate, based on an estimate of the number of referring GPs to the Centre, that the annual number of patients seen by referring GP's far exceed those cited by the DoH (1995). One would expect local and regional variations from the mean calculated by the DoH (which divided the annual number of cases by the number of GPs. As we will indicate later, our figures are consistent with estimates which indicate a higher than average incidence of breast cancer in the south east region of the United Kingdom. In order to establish this we propose to compare our own figures with those collected by the South Thames Region.

Information on patient volume is critical in the resource planning of services both at purchaser and provider level. This is useful in the following ways:-

- the number of cases diagnosed each year has implications for resource planning

- incidence rates for the catchment area in comparison with other units;

- prevalence patterns

- changes in volume may be associated with survival rates

- finally, volume data may also indicate epidemiological trends over time

What deductions can we make about the annual volume of patients seen from these two sources i.e. symptomatic and screen detected?

The West Sussex Breast Centre draws its patients from a catchment area which centres on Worthing with a population of 94000 to Shoreham Town (Adur District) to the east (population circa 58,000), and Arundel (Arun District) to the west (population 52,000). The catchment area to the north includes villages and towns including Storrington to Steyning located in the geographical district of North Downs (population circa 37,000). Based on this geographical area with a total population density of 241,000, and of adult women aged 16 and above at circa 70,000, one would expect to see a volume of patients at the breast cancer centre of circa 1,460. This is based on the Office of Population Census and Surveys (OPCS) calculations of cumulative rate (CR%) which is calculated by adding the age specific incidence rates for particular categories of age cohorts.

This unit operates a system where both cohorts of patients are seen at the West Sussex Breast Centre, by a specialist team. This contrasts with practice elsewhere and in non specialist units where cases are seen by a variety of surgeons. It is clear that a specialist unit will have higher numbers of patients. The population base of women over 16 years of age is 70,000 as of the 1994 electoral register. The number of patients referred to the unit on an annual basis is 1.2. per 1000 women. Compared to regional figures i.e. that of the South Thames which include the two Thames areas, the figures compare reasonably well. These figures when tested inferentially to determine whether they are significantly different by Chi Square tests yielded figures indicating that the volume of patients treated at Worthing is higher than expected. Table 1 below indicates the figures for each audit year for the respective cohorts since 1989.

Table 1: Breakdown of annual figures of patients seen via the two cohorts

Year	Cohort 1	Cohort 2	Totals
1989 (1)	8	13	21
1990 (2)	11	44	55
1991 (3)	94	95	189
1992 (4)	107	81	188
1993 (5)	144	100	244
1994 (6)	159	79	238
1995 (7)	178	104	282
1996 (8)	118	96	214

These figures are displayed graphically in Figure 8 below

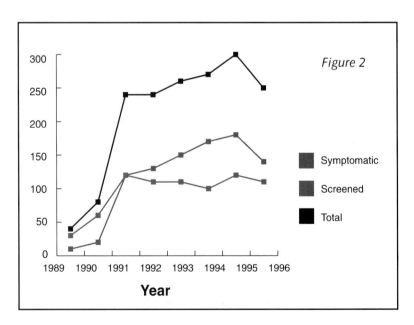

Figure 2

These figures reflect a lower base line during the initial period. This is because screening started in August 1989 and did not reach full implementation until the end of 1990. In addition the reorganisation of the symptomatic service was not completed until 1991. In subsequent years one would expect to achieve a stable number of symptomatic cancers. It is predicted that there should be a gradual fall in the numbers of cancers detected as a result of screening, as more women enter the screening programme. The Health of the Nation (HON) figures show an annual % increase year on year until 1995 of an average of 4.8%.

The volume of cases seen at the WSBC shows an increase when compared to other provider sites in the south east. These figures are indicated below in a summary extracted from the Thames Cancer Registry details.

Table 2: Thames Cancer Registry details of breast surgery volume at 4 provider sites

	1992	1993	1994	1995
Chichester	85	43	50	41
Eastbourne	125	94	64	82
Hastings	96	90	89	60
Worthing	170	184	196	171
	(188)	(244)	(238)	(282)

The figures in Table 2 indicate substantial variation in activity at the respective sites. The figures, shown in brackets, for Worthing are our own updated data.

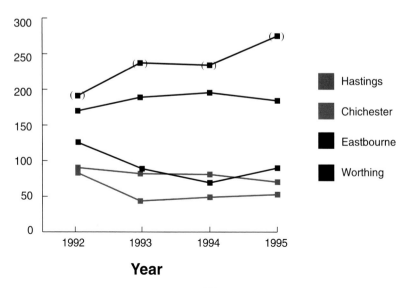

Consequences of volume for workload

The issue of volume has in addition attracted further importance given recent attempts by professional bodies and clinical interests groups at auditing workload performance, at both regional and national levels. Examples here include the audits conducted at regional level of surgical workload performance in the Thames region as well as the Hospital Surgical Workload returns. An attempt to map these figures has been made and are outlined in Tables 3,4, and 6.

Table 3: Breast Surgery Consultant Workload in SWT

	No of Consultants	Median No of cases per consultant	No. of Consultants at Worthing	Median no of cases at Worthing
Mastectomy	48	3	2	8
Plastic surgery of Breasts	18	0.26	1	0.6

Table 4 : Hospital Workload of Breast Surgery in SWT

	No of Cases	No of Hospitals	No of Specialist centres	No of Hos. with< 10 procedures	No of Hos. with< 25 procedures	No of procedures at Worthing(1995)
Mastectomy	553	14	3	1	6	282
Plastic surgery of Breasts	335	8		5	5	46

Table 5: Breast Surgery Volume in SWT

	Numbers in SWT	Crude SWT rate per million	Crude Worthing rate per million
Mastectomy	553	184	210
Plastic Surgery	335	111	118

Furthermore, the changes arising out of the NHS and Community Care Act (1990) specifically that of G.P Fund Holding Scheme, may have an impact on the volume of patients seen. This is likely because fund holding GP's may be exercising greater use of their funding base to refer their patients for specialist services at the centre. Simultaneously it is arguable that sustained efforts by the specialist groups including BBG and BASO in educating clinicians about the value and role of specialist breast centres, may as a consequence result in increased referrals to such centres.

Further analysis of the Volume of Patients Seen

The pattern of screen detected patients can be analysed for convenience along the parameters used by BASO (1996) which includes:-

- number of women with invasive cancer
- number of women with non-invasive cancer
- number of women who had a pre-operative diagnosis
- number of therapeutic operations
- number of women in whom nodal status is known
- number of women with surgical treatment
- number of women with conservation surgery
- relationship between mastectomy to tumour size
- treatment approach; mastectomy versus conservation by tumour size
- percentage of treatment not recorded; cases per surgeon

Our data sets provide entries which will enable us to carry out this analysis specifically in respect of our own cohort at a later date. In addition our findings will be pooled with entries from other national centres so as to attempt multi-site comparisons.

Age Characteristics Of The Two Cohorts

Breast Screening programmes target women aged 50 to 64. The underlying assumption is that this age group is more susceptible to breast cancer problems as well as more likely to accept mammographic screening. Figure 4 below indicates the breakdown of the age categories of the two groups.

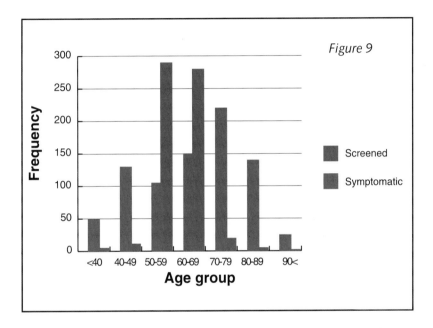

Figure 9

We wanted to explore the relationship of age at the time of diagnosis. At face value such an assessment may help to indicate to us whether there are any patterns which are associated between the modes of referrals and age categories. This specific indicator is, however dependent on two considerations. The first of which is contingent upon the date recorded by the General Practitioner (GP) at the time of consultation. This may however differ from the date that is recorded at the time of actual radiographic or histological or fine needle aspiration confirmation. This can be accounted for, save in emergency situations, by the natural delay which occurs between GP consultation and the date of appointment at the specialist centre.

As is indicated in figure 4, the patterns related to age characteristics reflect an average and predicted range of volume of patients of all age groups in cohort 1, with the highest concentration of around 215 patients in the 70-79 age group. When patients in this group are added to those in the 80-89 age category, it becomes evident that these overall numbers reflect the expected locality based increase in the over 70 age group. Whilst this volume of patients will obviously incur additional resource demands at a local level, it is likely that this trend will continue on a national basis as the number of patients in the over 70 age groups increase. It should be stressed that the increased numbers in these age categories are not related to recurrence or accounting by finished consultant episodes. A possible explanation is linked to the increased likelihood of breast cancer with progressive age.

As was expected, the screen detected cohort reflected age related concentration of numbers in age categories 50-59 and 60-69 accounting for the largest volumes of almost 300 subjects in each case. Furthemore the numbers are equally distributed between the two age cohorts and are not unexpected. The volumes audited based on age characteristics reflect patterns that we would expect in the South East, which on balance has a higher than average incidence of breast cancer. From both a purchaser and provider perspective, the incidence of breast cancer in the over 50's in the locality reflects predicted crude age related expectancies and as such is an effective lever in contracting for services in this category.

Some Questions That We Can Reflect Upon
In Respect Of Age Characteristics

a) What lessons could be identified in respects of age related incidence?

b) Are there significant differences between age cohorts in screened versus symptomatic cohorts?

c) Are there implications based on the incidence and age related trends that should be of concern to the provider centre?

With respect to diagnosis date we were interested to assess whether any differences existed between Cohorts 1 and 2. In other words, were there differences in the speed or timing of diagnosis between the two groups of patients? Furthermore, if there were differences, what patterns did these differences reflect? Firstly it has to be noted that we calculated these times in actual calendar months. The mean values for each cohort category has been subjected to one way ANOVA as a means of establishing the difference, if any, between the two groups, as significant differences emerged.

The findings derived from this analysis indicate that there were no discernible patterns in diagnosis times and we therefore concluded that there are no significant differences in diagnosis date recordings.

Practice Implications

Evidently, General Practitioners and their clients will be interested in the implications of the two referral route ways and their consequences for treatment. They will be reassured by the findings of this audit in terms of service responsiveness against consumer/patients expectations, given the gravity of patients' diagnostic concerns.

Last Seen Date

This issue will be discussed fully later on as it is centrally related to treatment approaches and considerations. As it reflected the second of the data sets in the audit it is considered here for convenience. This data item simply records the date and as a consequence the derived interval between diagnosis, treatment and last consultation with a clinician. The interval derived therefore enables one to calculate the time from treatment to recurrence free period. This issue is of importance in assessing the relationship between tumour types, treatment and recurrence free periods as well as age related factors.

Raw data for last seen date are derived through calculations of dates in calendar months rounded up to the nearest week. These figures have then been subjected to tests assessing mean differences. The overall patterns represents variable time differences across both cohorts. One can therefore conclude at this stage that there are no associated patterns between these issues. However, we will consider more critically the relationship between last seen dates and tumour characteristics at a later point in this analysis.

Survival Period

This data set represents the interval in months since diagnosis date and the last seen date. As is obvious this data set therefore extends the information given in data set no. 2 i.e. Last Seen Date. It, however, parcels out the calculation in a manner which allows more sensitive analysis of recurrence free intervals i.e. survival period to be made. This issue is tangentially related to the wider issue of incidence of breast cancer as a whole and it is to this issue that we now direct attention. We will later return to examine survival outcomes and associated issues.

Incidence of Breast cancer in South Thames Region.

The Thames Cancer Registry Statistics (1995) indicates that there has been a gradual increase in relative survival rate since 1960. In effect the percentage increase of survival rate has risen from around 56% in 1960 to around 70% in 1989. These figures do have implications for the volume of patients seen in two respects. Firstly as Chamberlain et al (1993) have indicated, the percentage of breast cancer patients diagnosed has increased because of uptake of breast screening services. Specifically, the figures indicate a 1% average annual increase during the 1980-1987 period. However since 1988-1990, breast cancer incidence rates have quadrupled to 4% on average. Chamberlain et al (1993) account for such an increase as a direct consequence of the targeting for screening purposes of the 50-64 years age group. Indeed these figures are even higher in the South East of England which reflects an increase of around 18% than that expected prior to the screening programme. Increased uptake of screening has therefore led to an increase of diagnosis of breast cancer cases. Advances in treatment as well as early detection may in combination be having an impact upon survival rates. The number of patients seen as represented in the volumes of cases in these two cohorts may be an artefact of those factors as is outlined in Cancer Registry figures below.

Table 6: Summary Of Age Standardised Incidence By District

Location	No of Cases	Age standardised rate
East Sussex	557	84.0
West Kent	594	80.6
East Kent	401	73.2
Bromley	176	74.5
Bexley & Greenwich	247	79.4
Lambeth,Southwark & Lewisham	344	70.7
Croydon	196	75.8
Merton,Sutton & Wandsworth	346	74.3
Kingston & Richmond	197	82.6
Western Surrey	400	78.1
Eastern Surrey	268	78.6
West Sussex	469	69.8

Tumour Categories

Histological analysis as a consequence of diagnosis allows tumour types to be isolated into a number of categories viz.:- lobular, tubular, ductal, rare as well as whether they are located in situ or are invasive. The frequency count of these types may indicate as to whether, given the volume of patients seen in the respective cohorts, any particular type has occurred more than is statistically expected.

Our data sets allowed us to list cancer types as one of three categories viz.:-

- Ductal
- Lobular
- Tubular

Furthermore we were able to record whether they were confined to ducts or lobules only, and as such, two other sub categories were noted i.e. Ductal Carcinoma in-situ (DCIS) or Lobular Carcinoma in-situ (LCIS). The latter of these is a marker for the presence of an invasive cancer, either at the present time or in the future. This marker therefore enabled us to determine whether or not patients should be followed up and screened for cancer. In this way we were able to record frequency data for each type of carcinoma. As some forms of cancers affecting the breast are particularly rare, we allowed an entry cell for noting the occurrence of "rare" carcinomas as well. Where such occurrence is further differentiated, our data sets allowed for brief comments to be added to the spread sheet.

Table 7 below summarises the frequency in numbers of each type of breast cancer for each of the two cohorts.

	Cohort 1 (Symptomatic)	Cohort 2 (Screened)
Lobular	88	54
Tubular	23	37
Ductal	557	397
DCIS	45	100
LCIS	02	00
Rare	40	15

As can be seen in these figures, there are no well defined patterns to the frequency of the respective groups of cancer types These figures were then tested inferentially so as to assess whether the observed frequencies are significantly different from those that can be expected statistically. A Chi - square series of test were conducted on each type on their own and for each cohort respectively. The results are summarised in Table 8 below.

Table 8

Type	Observed cases	Chi-square value	Significance
Tubular	65	1182.8099	.000
Lobular	137	935.4640	.000
Rare	55	1219.4556	.000

These figures indicate that the observed frequencies of both Tubular as well as Lobular breast cancers are statistically significant. The incidence is furthermore higher than that expected. It should also be noted, that the incidence of these two types have certain distinct patterns as each type goes in different directions.

The difference noted in the incidence between tubular and lobular cancer in the two cohorts is not unexpected. This is because lobular cancers are often radio lucent and therefore go undetected at screening mammography. Tubular cancers are often picked up by mammographic characteristics and their natural history supports the length bias. Similarly, incidence figures of rare cancers also achieved significant values. We would wish to compare these frequencies with the data derived from other centres and for that matter from regional or national pools of subjects.

Size Of Tumours In mm

We were interested in exploring the patterns that exist (if any) between tumour types and size of tumours. Our audit allowed for the entry of data sets which simply recorded the size in millimetres of tumours found at time of surgery, or in some inoperable cases, estimates based on radiological assessments. This indicator enabled us to explore patterns and relationship among a series of factors including age and size of tumour. Here the assumption is that older women may have tumours which are far more advanced than those in younger women. This issue may also be compounded by the time factor i.e. screen detected women are naturally identified earlier and will thus present with smaller tumour at diagnosis. This contrasts sharply with women who have self examined, found a lump and then sought GP consultation. We were interested in exploring whether any patterns existed between the size of tumour and the respective categories of tumour types and this issue will be subjected to a range of inferential tests.

Grades of tumours

The data for the respective cohorts were analysed in terms of entries for grades of tumours in each of the cohorts. Four codes of grades were recorded as follows:

blank = no entry made
1 = grade 1
2 = grade 2
3 = grade 3

The entries for the respective grades are summarised below:

Cohort	Blank 0	Grade 1	Grade 2	Grade 3
Screen detected	186	136	209	81
Symptomatic	216	138	272	193

The pattern for these grades are obviously variable and reflect statistical differences only in Grades 2 and 3; with higher incidence of these in the symptomatic cohort.

The incidence of rare tumours (n=40 and representing 5%) in the symptomatic cohort was slightly more than that occuring (n=15 at 2.5%) in the screen detected cohort.

Nodes positive

A similar type of analysis was carried out for the volume of nodes found to be positive for cohort 1 compared with that of cohort 2. Nodes positive was also statistically significant between the two cohorts (F=53.798; p=0.000) with a higher incidence in the symptomatic group.

Based on our own analysis, it is apparent that 84.6% of women were diagnosed as having an invasive type of tumour as opposed to 10.2.% who have a non-invasive type.

BASO (1996) survey gathered data from 9 regions in England and 1 from Wales. Of these, 4 RHA's returned figures that categorised diagnosis in terms of both invasive and non-invasive types of tumours. These findings are indicated below.

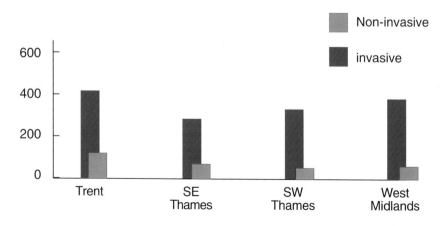

On Treatment Approaches

The Thames Cancer Registry figures provide overviews of cancer treatment in terms of the number of patients who are treated with chemotherapy, radiotherapy and surgery. The overview for the 1992 figures which were published in 1995, are outlined in Table 9 below.

Table 9: Details of treatment patterns for cancers in general across the Thames Regions

District	CMX	%	DXT	%	Surgery	%	No treatment	%	Total
North Thames	6811	38	5594	31	11280	63	2317	13	17929
South Thames	7142	36	5668	29	12059	61	3021	15	19752
South East	14480	37	11618	30	24235	62	5667	14	39251
Worthing	174	12	570	40	546	48	56	0	1431

These figures indicate some different patterns as far as breast cancer care is concerned and more specifically those located within a specialist breast cancer centre. At face value the use of chemotherapy on its own is low in comparison with the trend for cancer in general, but allied to figures of patients who have been treated with Tamoxifen (at 1297 recorded cases representing some 90% of all patients), the figures are not surprisingly high. Similarly, the use of radiotherapy in breast cancer care shows an expectedly high percentage. This pattern can be explained in context of adjuvant therapy which represents a combination of modes of treatment. In general cancer care surgical intervention is used across some 60% of cases as compared to some 48% in breast cancer care. This figure includes circa 38% of patient who are treated by a mastectomy either as a first, or in some cases, a second operation.

We would wish to isolate the age related weighting of these figures and a number of questions come to mind as follows:-

- to what extent is treatment approach dependent on age considerations?
- to what extent is treatment associated with type of cancer?
- to what extent are lumpectomies and mastectomies age related?

More topical in context of the referral patterns used here is that of the nature of differences, if any, in the treatment approaches used for the two cohorts? The frequency count for treatment approaches across the two cohorts are summarised below.

Table 10: Summary of treatment across cohorts

	CMX	DXT	Mastectomy
Cohort 1	135	284	401
Cohort 2	39	286	145

On face value alone it is obvious that these frequency counts represent a difference in treatment approach save for the use of radiotherapy which appears even across both groups. Symptomatic patients would appear to have been exposed to more chemotherapy and mastectomy in comparison with screen detected patients.

The last of these questions was further tested in context of whether Cohort 1 and Cohort 2 differed statistically in terms of treatment approaches. In order to test these assumptions we conducted a series of t-tests for independent samples representing Cohorts 1 and 2 respectively. With regards to the use of chemotherapy, for instance, our analysis indicates a t value of -6.20 with two tailed significance of 0.000, thus indicating a difference in the use of chemotherapy for the two cohorts. However, as had been indicated earlier, the use of chemotherapy together with Tamoxifen makes analysis difficult. Similar significant values were derived for mastectomy.

There are a number of possible explanations which may account for these differences. To begin with, we are aware of the inherent differences that arise as a consequence of the nature and severity of the breast cancer that the patient has presented with. It is likely that screen detected patients may be presenting at diagnosis, tumours which are smaller and of better prognosis.

With regards to the management of these cases one can raise questions about the number of patients with surgical management and in particular mastectomy who received post-mastectomy radiation. As Fowble (1997) has indicated, the role of post mastectomy adjuvant radiotherapy in the treatment of operable breast carcinoma remains controversial. A number of studies (Griem et al 1987, Grohm et al 1987, Klefstron et al 1987, Velez-Garcia 1992, Ragaz et al 1993, 1996) have demonstrated a decrease of incidence in loco-regional recurrence in patients receiving adjuvant chemotherapy with radiotherapy. Fowble, however, argues that there are considerable variations in outcomes as well as differences in findings based on how the studies i.e. clinical trials have been designed. She cites the case of the Eastern Co-operative Oncology Group (ECOG) randomised trial of post-mastectomy patients in the areas of design, heterogeneity of study populations, sample size, protocol of design, as well as statistical analysis as sources of distortion and bias.

Fisher, Anderson and Redmond (1995) carried out a study which aimed to compare treatment outcomes in women undergoing total mastectomy with that of lumpectomy with or without radiotherapy (RT). The data were derived from a prospective audit based on a 12 year period of follow up, involving 88 centres in North America and 1 centre in Australia. The sample consisted of 2163 women with breast cancer of < 4 cm. Their results indicated that after a 12 year follow up period the survival rates for mastectomy were 60%, lumpectomy 58%, and lumpectomy plus RT, 62%. These figures achieved significant values between mastectomy and lumpectomy. Disease free survival and distant disease free survival rates did not differ among treatment groups. The researchers further reported that the 12 year cumulative incidence of ipsilateral breast tumour recurrence for patients who received lumpectomy alone was 35% compared to 10% for those receiving lumpectomy plus RT. Of some interest here is a comparison of the general treatment patterns for women treated at West Sussex Breast Centre. The five year mortality figure for symptomatic patients is 16% and for Screen Detected subjects the figure is 4%.

Similarly, findings reported by the Early Breast Cancer Trialist Collaborative Group (1995), indicated that if the "local disease is completely excised, the extent of surgery does not affect survival rates in women with early stage breast cancer" (page 118). The addition of radiotherapy to surgery reduces local recurrence by two-thirds, but does not affect survival. These findings were deduced from a meta-review of 36 studies comparing surgery alone with the same type of surgery with radiotherapy in 17,273 women.

Surgery compared to same surgery with RT indicated that mortality was 41% for surgery alone and 40% for surgery plus RT (p = 0.3). In the same review, 28 studies provided information on the causes of death. The findings indicated that more women who received RT died of non-breast cancer causes, than did women who received surgery alone (8% vs 6%; p=0.002). Fewer women who received RT died of breast cancer than did women who received surgery alone (34% vs 37%: p = 0.031). Furthermore, 7% of women who received RT had local recurrences, compared with 20% who had surgery only. For studies assessing mastectomy compared to conserving surgery plus RT (9 studies) the groups did not differ for total mortality: 23% versus 23%. Similarly, Jacobsen, Danforth, Cowan et al (1996) reported findings supporting earlier studies which showed that radical mastectomy, and breast conserving surgery plus radiotherapy, had similar disease free survival rates in the early stages of cancer.

Questions to reflect upon in respect of variations in treatment

The audit findings have enabled us to consider:-

- are symptomatic patients treated differently, and if so for what reasons?

- are screen detected patients managed differentially because of the method of diagnosis?

- what implications for resource planning and management does the age related factor pose for breast cancer management locally?

Survival Issues

We have earlier alluded to the impact of survival rates on the volume of patients seen. Our data indicated that patients in the screen detected cohort experienced longer survival periods (measured in calendar months and calculated as the interval between diagnosis date to last seen date). The mean survival interval for this cohort was 30.2 months compared to 23.05 months for patients in the symptomatic group. This difference achieved significance levels with F=46.316; p=0.000).

Here, however, we wish to follow up this issue by assessing the impact that age and treatment may have upon survival. We note the extent to which this issue has been the subject of prior studies, most notably of which is that of Schrijvers (1995) who pointed out the connections between stage of diagnosis, age and socio-economic deprivation on survival rates. Furthermore, the OPCS findings of 1995 show a corresponding decline in deaths in the 50-69 year old age groups. Likewise, the Thames Cancer Registry findings show an increase in the 5 year relative survival rates for breast cancer patients in South Thames region. From an audit point of view it would be immensely useful to isolate the factors that are associated with survival rates. Our own cohorts are substantial enough for us to isolate these effects. There are, however, two points to make at the outset. We have not included socio-economic and other defining characteristics on our data sets and attempts to isolate these correlates now would be difficult as far as this retrospective audit is concerned. Furthermore, we are considering the issue of survival and quality of life associated with the over 80's as a separate study. In addition, we recognise that survival may be related to a host of other factors. At this stage, it is difficult to assess these factors in isolation. We therefore attempted to explore the relationship of a range of factors as are indicated below:-

Factor	Factor	Correlation Coefficient	Significance value
Age	second-op	r = -.1811	p = .000
DXT	second -op	r = -.0773	p = .003
CMX	Tamoxifen	r = -.0933	p = .000
DCIS	Tamoxifen	r = .0557	p = .035
DCIS	second-op	r = .1608	p = .000
Lobular	second-op	r = .0855	p = .001
Mastectomy	Tamoxifen	r = .0895	p = .001

These findings indicate that a relationship exists between a number of variables and whilst they do not establish cause and effect type relationships, they are none the less indicative of a number of interesting patterns. For instance, it is obvious that a relationship exists between age and second-operation. Increasing age correlates positively with having a second operation. On the other hand, attempts at breast conservation result in more second operations in younger women to produce clear margins. Axillary surgery, also, is often carried out as a second procedure. With a histological pre-operative diagnosis, the axilla can be dealt with at the time of primary surgery and the numbers of second operations fall. Furthermore, positive correlations are evident between cohort groups and DXT (r=.1382;p=000); cohort groups and CMX (r = .1531;p =.000) and cohort groups and mastectomy (r = .2574; p = .000). Whilst correlations do not indicate any causal relationship, they do suggest some interesting questions for further research study.

On affected sides, residual tumours and vascular invasion

Data entries for these three aspects of breast cancer were analysed to examine differences or similarities in the two cohorts. With regards to whether there were differences in either left or right sided tumours, the data indicated that there was no statistical difference in sides affected. There was a greater incidence of vascular invasion in the symptomatic group with a mean incidence of 0.2 compared to a mean of 0.03 in the screen detected cohort. These differences achieved significance levels (F=140.344; p=0.000). Similarly, patients in the symptomatic cohort also presented with a higher incidence of residual tumours (F=8.930; p=0.003).

Interval data

At the present time there is a good deal of interest in the incidence of interval cancers, particularly in patients in the screen detected cohort. Interval cancers, for the present, are regarded as those which appear between screening episode in women who have had normal screening. Figure 9 below indicates that the incidence occuring over the second course of screening of this audit study represents an interval rate of 52%.

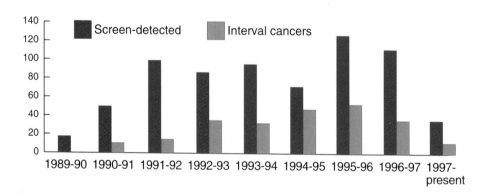

An audit of interval cancers is needed based on this graph. Things that need elucidating are: (i) time between last screening and diagnosis of interval cancer; (ii) tumour type - lobular carcinomas tend to be translucent; (iii) size and grade of tumour; (iv) nodal status.

This will be the subject of a separate study.

If one excludes the cases that can be identified retrospectively from screening mammograms, one is left with particular varieties of breast cancer, which may pose treatment considerations. A future study will examine these issues with reference to :-

- age of patient
- interval between screening and diagnosis
- type of tumour
- grade of tumour
- nodal status
- HRT status
- family history
- outcome

On death and mortality issues

Our data allowed us to code and then categorise entries based on cause of death:

- cause due to breast cancer (Code 1)
- cause unrelated to breast cancer (Code 2)
- cause unknown (Code 9)

Table 11 below, summarises the entries based on the above coding

Cohort	Code 1	Code 2	Code 9
Screen detected	06	05	—
Symptomatic	86	24	18

The figures represent 1% and 10.5% respectively of the sample size from each cohort. These findings, when tested inferentially indicate that there is a statistical difference between the two cohorts, with $F=124.670$; $p=0.000$.

Summary of audit findings

- over an 8 year period we have observed an increase in the volume of patients treated at the centre

- there are no significant differences in volume of patients seen between the screen detected and symptomatic cohorts, but the increase in volume does have resource planning implications

- age related characteristics and in particular increase in volume in the over 60 age category are higher than national norms

- The West Sussex Breast Centre treats a higher volume of breast cancer patients than other provider sites in the South Coast

- the length of survival experienced by screen detected patients is greater than that of symptomatic patients

- the observed frequencies for tubular, ductal and rare breast cancers are higher than that expected by chance

- screening successfully detects favourable cancers (tubular and grade 1) which contributes to length bias and improved survival of screen detected patients. This should also include a lead time bias over symptomatic patients

- symptomatic patients were more often treated with chemotherapy and mastectomy than screen detected patients

- there were higher incidence of vascular invasion and residual tumours in patients in the symptomatic than in the screen detected cohort .

Chapter 5

In previous chapters we have outlined accounts which provided detailed and comprehensive commentaries on the nature of audit. The principle and practice of audit were described to enable clinicians and practitioners to develop knowledge and understanding which they can apply to their own practice. In addition we have made a detailed case for the central role of audit in a research based culture and how it can be used to support research activities in relation to the development of evidence based practice in health care. Furthermore, we have demonstrated the natural link between audit and reflective practice. The latter approach, we argue, has the potential of promoting work based learning through reflection. We have located this on the continuum, spanning reflective practice at one end to empirical research at the other. In chapter three we discussed a range of issues pertaining to the development of an audit study and in Chapter 4 we have demonstrated how data gathered from our audit can be used to analyse and provide meaning on a range of topical aspects of breast cancer care.

In this final chapter we wish to discuss the relevance of these findings. We intend to highlight areas in which we are able to extend this study and to change current practice so as to enhance the nature of our work. We had earlier established the case that the most important aspect of an audit study is that in which change can be brought to bear on health care outcomes.

Lessons learnt from the conduct of the audit

It would have been a tremendous benefit for us to reflect on the outcomes of our work in a primary sense and to identify the central lessons attributable to our study. In reality, the nature and practice of, as well as the rationale for audits has changed considerably. Our audit has also been conducted in context of a range of other influencing factors and variables. In other words, some of the key lessons learnt are in part to do with our study. But they also result from influences emanating from other sources relating to the requirements and conditions in which audits are being conducted, here and elsewhere.

At the outset, we wish to reflect on the first and perhaps the most important consideration, that of the nature of the data sets that constitute the audit. As we have shown earlier there are a number of key indicators on which data must be gathered. It is evident from the data sets selected, that we have covered most of the important items necessary for meaningful and purposeful audit. We would like to reiterate those items here as follows:-

- *consultation times and diagnosis;*
- *range of diagnostic strategies;*
- *type, size and grade of tumours;*
- *location and affected side;*
- *treatment methods;*
- *nature of surgery;*
- *subsequent surgery as necessary;*
- *follow up care;*
- *survival rates;*
- *timing and causes of death;*
- *other comments .*

It is furthermore our contention that as is indicated in the BASO data sets, there are a number of items that are essential for data gathering for multi-site comparisons and research. We value the benefits that can accrue from multi-site comparison studies. Apart from locality based comparisons, such studies have value in epidemiological mapping to trace patterns and trends of incidence as well as on treatment outcomes. It may be necessary for a Clinical Trials Co-ordinator to be solely responsible for ensuring that comprehensive data are gathered for these purposes. However, it may be more beneficial that all practitioners who are involved in the diagnosis, treatment and follow up care of breast cancer patients be actively involved in gathering data that relate to the aspects for which they are responsible, so as to ensure that the task is both shared and owned. This strategy has the added advantage of ensuring that knowledge and understanding of the conduct of audit is developed by a wider array of personnel involved in clinical care of these patients. Those directly involved in gathering and collating data may likewise be able to reflect upon the value, relevance and parameters of the data gathered so as to ensure that they are able to act upon and bring about the desired change as is necessary. In this way, education, ownership and development of clinicians and therapy staff are addressed on an on-going basis.

We would argue that the items on which we have focused are important for our present purposes. But at the point of initial consultation and history taking, for example, additional data on demographics could be recorded in a standard format, as has been suggested by BASO. These data are simply forwarded to other clinicians as part of the normal referral process. We certainly support the need for additional data on demographics and recognise the central part that such data can serve in epidemiological and other analysis. In this regard we would envisage additional emphasis on:-

- *data sets on familial history;*
- *data sets on demographic factors;*
- *data sets on onset and presenting symptomatology;*
- *data sets on factors influencing consultation and referrals.*

One area that we would certainly need to examine and create a mechanism for data gathering is that which relates to the nature of support and counselling. In the BASO data set, information on the involvement and use of the breast cancer nurses and counsellors are explicitly addressed. We support these indicators and would like to promote this through the more systematic use of the breast care nurses within our own department.

This aspect will need pursuing in a manner which reflects the specific cultural aspects of the Centre in which we work, as well as matching the need for gathering data and service provisions which are consistent with the recommendations of BBG, BASO and of the quality criteria outlined in contracting specifications of commissioning authorities.

On the nature and value of psychological support

The issue of psychological, and perhaps more specifically, emotional support, has attracted considerable research attention and is the source of much audit activity over recent times as far as breast cancer care is concerned. Based on the work of a number of workers in this field including Orr (1986), Meyerowitz (1980), Delay (1991), Celikoglu (1995) and Fallowfield (1995), it is clearly established that psychological and emotional support provides substantial benefits to patients as they adjust to the diagnosis and treatment of their conditions. Whilst it is apparent that these benefits are possible, it is nonetheless necessary to note that emotional and psychological support have several levels of expression and one would need to be clear as to the diverse factors that may be operating here which can affect processes and outcomes in this field.

Consistent with this line of reasoning, Elal-Lawrence & Celikoglu (1995), for instance, have argued for the need to consider the ways in which psychological support has been operationalised. They suggested, for instance, that the dominant trend in operational definitions is that of referring to psychological support as "certain functions performed for a distressed individual". Whilst such definitions do not concern themselves with the sources or providers of such support in the first instance, they nonetheless discriminate in terms of the nature and form of support provided. Three distinct forms of functions are alluded to and include instrumental, emotional, as well as informational aid. Others such as Cobb (1976) argue that psychological support is usually manifest as information giving which leads individuals to believe that they are "cared for, are valued and that they are members of a network of communication". On the other hand, psychological support is seen by Barera (1986) as the direct action of others when they provide assistance to another person. Wortman (1984) suggested that emotional support is about having an opportunity to discuss feelings.

In the clinical situation and in breast cancer care in particular, emotional and psychological support together with information giving all serve a vital role in addressing patients' satisfaction with care. It is difficult to isolate the relative strengths of these respective elements but it is clear that information giving is now of central importance in the interaction between patients and clinicians. Timely, meaningful and direct information may therefore play an important role in alleviating patients' anxieties about their condition and as such can be seen as one level of support.

In cancer care, a number of studies including Taylor (1988), Orr (1986) and Fallowfield (1995) have explored the nature and value of psychological support in this context. Orr, for instance, has reported that open communication of feelings correlates with poor adjustment, in other words having the opportunity to discuss feelings openly may be beneficial in some ways but does not necessarily have an impact upon readjustment to the condition. However, when subjects were given the opportunity to discuss facts about their illness, the outcomes in terms of adjustment were far superior.

Naturally, questions about the source of support also warrant consideration as well. Dunkel-Schetter (1984) and Dakof & Taylor (1990) indicated that the spouse of the client and their immediate family are more important sources of support than others. Meyerowitz (1980) and Delay (1991) suggested that the support of the spouse in breast cancer care is of particular importance, especially behaviours where there is a positive emotional component. It can be argued however, that such support may be important at a particular time during the course of the patient's condition, at other periods different kinds of support or minimal amounts may be required. This point is borne out in a study by Dunkel-Schetter (1984) in which it is shown that the support and social interaction, or a lack of it, can be the cause of withdrawal and communication problems. Some patients reported feelings of rejection, withdrawal and other communication problems with close family members.

Elal-Lawrence & Celikoglu found that, in a sample of 72 women with breast cancer, the level of emotional support provided could be differentiated between that provided by spouses and by significant others. In effect, the researchers indicated that women who felt that "they could readily talk to their husbands about their illness and mutually share emotions seemed to be psychologically better adjusted". It would appear however that the direction of outcome is not clear and one would need to consider the extent to which other influencing factors are involved. In this study, 93% of women expressed the wish to talk about and discuss their breast cancer. 20% of this sample were unable to do so for a variety of reasons. This poses a number of questions about the difference between the desire to communicate and the actual practice of it.

Melville et al (1996) reviewed 13 studies which have explored the effects of choice on patients receiving either breast conserving surgery (BCS) or mastectomy (MST). Choice was fostered through the provision of information and support which patients were able to use in joint decision making about the type of treatment received. These studies were subjected to a meta-review, based on the Centre for Research Dissemination (CRD) guidelines for reviews. The main finding derived from this review indicates that psychotherapeutic counselling and educational intervention can improve the quality of life and may improve immune function which may have an effect of increased life expectancy in certain patients. The involvement of surgical and medical personnel in these roles needs further assessment. It would appear that the range of other staff providing this care which includes nurses, psychologists and psychiatrists are very much in the fore front in this service, possibly at the expense of specialist staff directly involved in breast cancer care. Whilst it is likely that emotional and informational aid may have a role to play in the total care of the patient, one should perhaps exercise some caution in making too grandiose claims, for as Melville et al pointed out, "a more definitive statement about the impact of psycho-social intervention is not possible because of the quality of studies" expressing doubts about the methodological integrity of studies conducted to explore these issues.

Obviously, the case for emotional and psychological support is becoming more compelling as one considers the emphasis that is now placed on holistic and complementary approaches to care. In this regard we are introducing additional audit indicators consistent with those proposed by BASO as well as extending the range of items on pyschological and emotional support. However, we are also aware that data of a qualitative nature on such items are more difficult to record. Breast cancer specialist nurses can fulfil a vital role in this aspect of data gathering.

Implications of audit workload

Our data sets have been compiled on an ongoing basis by two of us. We would stress that at the time of initiating this audit study in 1989, there was an absence of regional or for that matter, national guidelines that could have been used to inform the conduct and design of this study. We have therefore learnt from our attempt at both devising and executing the audit. Moreover, we are encouraged by the consistency of the core data sets that we have incorporated in the audit with those recommended recently by national groups including BBG and BASO, as well as by regional/local efforts as suggested by Garvigan (1996). Through the conduct of the audit we have accrued learning on audit per se as well as on methodology.

The experiences derived have also enabled us to refine our technique of data gathering. For instance, one of us has now perfected a technique which allows for systematic data recording, during clinics or after each surgical episode. The use of a lap top computer and familiarity with EXCEL spreadsheets has been beneficial in more ways than one. We have now also developed a system of cross checking of entries to enhance inter-observer agreement with case notes and other documented sources. We continue to reflect upon this process in terms of its effectiveness and efficiency in the gathering of data. It is obvious that as we continue to refine this system of working we will be in a position to advise on savings in terms of time and effort to other personnel involved. More importantly, we will be able to act as consultants in terms of assistance, support and as a resource to other colleagues in the development of effective audit systems and protocol. This is consistent with our strategy of learning about audit through reflective practice. We are, therefore, learning from our clinical actions in a manner which is consistent with the values and characteristics of professional development now being promoted by the Royal Colleges and the Research and Development strategy of the NHSE.

Reflection on Symptomatic and Screen detected patients

Our present mode of operation is based on two types of referral of patients, i.e. those being referred by their General Practitioners as well as those from the Breast Screening Programme. The pattern and number of symptomatic referrals may be influenced by two factors viz. volume, which may be subjected to slight reductions as more cases are screen detected and the other may be due to the mechanism of G.P fund holding which may create a slight increase in referrals by these practices. At a later stage, one may wish to focus on the impact of fund holding on referral patterns to the centre in respect of breast cancer care.

We have indicated in Chapter 4 that the volume of screen detected patients seen on a twelve month basis is levelling out. Despite fluctuations in earlier years of the audit, the figures are still comparable to predicted estimates, given the screening population of the locality.

On the notion of follow up

The audit data sets that we have devised allow scope for the recording of information on follow up. Specifically this data set relates to the recording of time in terms of calendar months that marks the total length of time (LAST SEEN DATE) since the patient was seen by the specialist team. Follow up care is seen as a standard practice and an area which is also monitored for a variety of reasons. These figures serve two purposes. On the one hand they provide a tracking system in order to enable us to plan follow up appointments and visits. On the other, they serve as a useful base on which to calculate survival periods and patterns. They provide, for instance, a system which enables us to calculate the percentage of patients on 5 years or 10 years survival periods.

From these calculations one can identify specific lessons in terms of whether there are differences in survival rates and patterns between the two cohorts, and if so, what are the nature and consequences of such patterns? Furthermore, what mechanism could one deploy from a resource utilisation perspective to maximise follow up outcomes? As we have inferred earlier, there are direct advantages in terms of treatment outcomes when breast cancer care is managed by specialist centres. What does the evidence suggest with respect to follow up care?

Based on two major sets of studies the findings would suggest that follow up care could be shared with general practitioners without any consequential diminution of quality outcomes. For instance, a British study conducted by Grundfield et al (1996) of a randomised controlled trial comparing the outcomes of follow up carried out by general practitioners to that by specialist breast cancer specialists, reported that there were no differences in duration on quality of life. Furthermore, follow up provided by general practitioners was deemed to be acceptable by both patients and clinicians alike. A review study conducted by Italian clinicians (GIVIO investigators 1994), and Rosselli del Turco et al (1994) reported no differences in 5 year survival (OR 1.03; 95% CI, 0.82 to 1.30) or health related quality of life measures. These findings were derived from a study between patients who were allocated to a group receiving intensive surveillance in contrast to a control group who were seen as often by doctors, but in whom tests were only carried out when the patients reported problems or symptoms. Finally, one may also draw some additional conclusions about the timing and value of follow up based on the findings reported by Wakefield and Powis (1995) who assessed the extent of routine follow up of patients undergoing excision biopsy in order to confirm benign disease (BBD). The findings here indicate that routine follow up of such patients "can safely be avoided if there is a satisfactory protocol which is understood by the patients and their GPs". Our follow up at the present time, is mammographic which may be more useful. Lifetime follow up at the centre allows accurate assessment of outcomes and provides a pool of patients for entry into trials.

Reflections on the Management of Breast Cancer

The data that we have gathered have facilitated a range of analyses on management approaches to breast cancer care. Specifically, we have considered patterns and volume of diagnostic and management approaches and treatment outcomes as they relate to survival rates. Based on the evidence derived, we are able to draw a number of conclusions. Firstly though, a consideration on diagnostic management.

We have analysed the patterns and outcomes of diagnosis at the centre based around the established practice of triple assessment i.e. a combination of clinical examination, mammography and fine needle aspiration. We are aware of the evidence derived from the review carried out by Butler et al (1990) which points to the value of triple assessments as being consistently more sensitive than any single form of diagnostic approach. They are more likely to diagnose 95%-100% of cancers when one or more of the diagnostic outcome are positive. We are fully aware of the value derived from a combination of the diagnostic findings of all three aspects, whether positive or negative, as providing a probability of around 99% of the certainty of the outcome. The fact that all three aspects of diagnosis can be carried out at the time of a single visit to the centre makes for a speedy diagnosis as well as being convenient for the patient. Furthermore, referral patterns from general practitioners may well be subjected to the kind of filtering system in which cases are classified as "urgent", "soon" or "routine" as has been described by Marsh and Archer (1996). In this study the researchers described how information derived from the general practitioner letter was graded as per the above three categories. From a total of 496 referrals, 94 were classed as " urgent", 186 as "soon" and 216 as "routine". The grading scheme was found to be valid in that of the 56 patients of the total sample found to have had a carcinoma, 41(73%) of the patients were drawn from the urgent group, 11 (19.6%) were from the category graded "soon" and 4(7.1%) were drawn from the routine group. The authors indicated that all the cancers in the routine group were "coincidental findings". It is evident that as volume patterns of referrals change, systems and mechanisms such as this could be employed as a basis of ensuring speedy diagnosis and treatment.

Although we have audited the timing of these tests in order to provide a reference point to calculate time intervals between diagnosis and last seen date which would determine survival outcomes, we would need to audit patient satisfaction with diagnostic arrangements as well as to examine whether there are patterns in the outcomes of the diagnostic tests. This will also enable us to test the basis of our diagnostic outcomes against findings such as those reported by Butler et al (1990). This will aid decision making with respect to cost effectiveness of the respective tests as well as on considerations about the use of surgical biopsy etc.

Empirical findings have substantially aided our decision making with regards to management approaches to breast cancer care. For instance it is now well established that management strategies of breast cancer are related to survival outcomes as has been reported by Atkins et al (1972) and Axelson et al (1992). Furthermore as was reported by Sainsbury et al (1995) patients who were treated by breast cancer specialists, i.e. those who saw more than 30 new cases a year had a better survival rate than those who were treated by surgeons who saw less than that number per year. With regards to actual surgical procedure of choice, studies including those of Veronesi et al (1981) and Fisher et al (1985) have reported findings indicating conservative surgery combined with radiotherapy produces local control of tumours and survival outcomes similar to selected patients having mastectomy.

Reflections on professional development through reflective practice and audit

We have demonstrated through the conduct of this study how our clinical practice could be developed through the use of reflective practice, audit, and of promoting a research based culture within the clinical environment. Moreover, the issues that we have audited have resulted in changes in some aspects of our practice; in other areas we have begun to ask additional questions that may stimulate empirical research work. In all of these areas it is evident that audit, improvements to practice and more effective use of resources are all part and parcel of professional practice. We therefore wish to focus on a number of aspects pertaining to professional development issues that may inform our future practice as well as that of other clinician and practitioners.

Whilst we have been advocating the case for reflective practice and audit as well as empirical research as a basis of enhancing patient care, questions as to the most effective method of improving professional practice and patient outcomes are continually being raised by clinicians, educators and researchers. For instance, in a review conducted by Davies et al in 1996, a number of 99 studies were evaluated as their impact and resultant change on health care practice. 55 of these studies assessed the practice of internists, 35 studies assessed the work of family physicians and 34 focused on residents. 75 of the studies related to practice in out-patient settings.

The researchers reported that of the 99 interventions, 62% showed improvements in more than one major outcome. 70% of interventions showed improvement in physician behaviour and 48% showed improvement in health care outcomes. The findings also indicated that interventions using two or more strategies are more frequently effective than those using 1 strategy. the authors were able to suggest that " individualised, practice based interventions are more effective at changing physicians behaviour than are traditional, didactic large group interventions".

The audit continues to cause us to reflect upon our every day actions. Our approach to treatment is being informed by the learning experiences derived through reflective practice. As developments on protocols and systems unfold within the field, we are able to incorporate such advances in order to enhance our clinical work. It is evident that a good deal of insight is gained from the hands on approach we initiated in 1989. Recently, we have been able to build on the advice of the BBG and BASO. The standardisation of data sets introduced by BASO for breast cancer audit has enabled us to identify other parameters that will impact upon the total care provided by patients. Through reflection on our work and the conduct of the audit, we have become more aware of research in the field. This has provided the impetus for us to become more active in the use of and engagement with research. The series of benefits derived from reflective practice, audit and now research are enabling us to pursue evidence based practice.

APPENDIX 1.

STANDARDS FOR AUDIT

These should be based on national guidelines. There is now considerable agreement on the quality standards which should be covered if not the outcome measures which are actually achievable. It is important to reach agreement on what measures are to be audited and analysed before the minimum dataset and database are designed.

8.1 Structural Measures Relating to Organisation of Breast Service

An annual return could include the composition of the Breast Care Team with details of specialisation and training and sessional commitments for the various staff. Facilities available on site with age and condition of equipment such as ultrasound and mammography machines should also be listed. Other institutional measures would include ability of Radiology and Pathology Services conforming to NHSBSP QA Standards. This would enable comparison with the prospective audit of the care of individual women.

8.2 Process Measures to Include in Prospective Audit

- Timescale of process from referral to treatment (or reassurance if all attenders included).

- Number of patient visits prior to diagnosis

- Proportion of pre-operative diagnoses for palpable lesions (BASO suggest 90%).

- Numbers of therapeutic operations

- Pathological size and grade of lesion recorded in all cases. Where surgery is deferred for chemotherapy, mammographic size must be recorded instead

- Proportion of invasive cancers with known nodal status

- Proportion of cases where diagnosis and treatment plan discussed at multidisciplinary review meeting

- Proportion of cases where a Breast Care Nurse is available to see the woman both pre-operatively and post-operativelt

- Patient involvement in choice of treatment
- Radiotherapy
  - offered
  - given
  - timescale

- Endocrine therapy

- Chemotherapy
  - offered
  - given
  - timescale

- Proportion of cases where trial eligibility and entry are established

- Outcome measure
  - repeat surgery (e.g. to clear margins)
  - complications
  - lymphoedema
  - local recurrence ⎫
  - regional recurrence ⎬ minimisation vs detection
  - contralateral breast cancers
  - metastases
  - death

8.3 Process measurement to include at some future date

In no particular order:

- ease of referral/interface with primary care
- psychological support and supply of relevant information
- radiotherapy fractionation policies
- prosthesis service
- palliative care
- If FNA samples adequate
- appropriate treatment for DCIS

8.4 Outcome Indications

- morbidity (QOL)
- mortality
- satisfaction

APPENDIX 2: BASO DATA SET

Data set for collection (subject to modification during the pilot phase)

1 BASIC INFORMATION

Name: ....

Address & Postcode: ....

....

....

Telephone number: ....

NHS Number ....

Date of Birth ..../....../.......

Marital status .... M / S / D / W / Unknown

NHS Breast Screening Programme Number ....

GP & Address ....

....

....

Breast Unit / Hospital. ....

Patient s Hospital Number ....

Consultant responsible
for surgery ....

Consultant responsible
for radiotherapy ....

Radiotherapy centre ....

Consultant responsible
for systemic adjuvant therapy ....

2 REFERRAL AND ATTENDANCE

How was the patient referred? ....

1 = by a GP   2 = from NHSBSP

Screen no ....

3 = other screening   3 = other referral

State ....

Date of referral (letter, phone, fax etc) ..../....../.......

At the time of referral, was this deemed urgent
by the surgeon? (i.e before seeing the patient) ....

1 = No   2 = Yes   9 = Not prioritised

Date first seen at out-patient clinic . . . . / . . . . / . . . .

Past History

Relevant Family History . . . .

                                                    1 = No   2 = Yes

Breast   . . . .
Ovarian   . . . .
Previous Breast Cancer . . . .

                                                    1 = No   2 = Yes

Date   . . . . / . . . . / . . . .
R / L / Bilateral   . . . .
Ovarian Cancer   . . . .

                                                    1 = No   2 = Yes

Date   . . . ./. . . . . ./. . . . . . .
Other breast operation . . . .

                                                    1 = No   2 = Yes

Date   . . . ./. . . . . ./. . . . . . .
Menopausal Status   . . . .

                                     1 = Pre-   2 = Post-   3 = Peri-

Taking HRT?   . . . .

                                                    1 = No   2 = Yes

Clinical Presentation
1. None   4. Changed   7. Nipple Pain
2. Lump   5. Discharge with blood 8. Cosmetic
3. Dimple   6. Discharge no blood   9. Other

Clinical findings
Right . . . . (size . . . . mm)   Left . . . . (size . . . . mm)
0 = No palpable lump   3 = Palpable Lump
1 = Pagets, no lump   4 = Lesion with infiltration, ulcer, etc
2 = Nodular area, no lump   9 = Other

Investigations
Mammography   . . . . Y / N
Ultrasound   . . . . Y / N
FNA cytology   . . . . Y / N
Wide bore needle biopsy . . . . . . Y / N

3 RADIOLOGY

Mammography

Name of radiologist	. . . .	
Hospital	. . . .	
Date of report	........./....../.......	
Side	Right	Left
Mammographic sign	. . . .	
Radiology confidence	. . . .	
Mammographic size	. . . .	
Localisation	. . . . (Y/N)	

Mammograpic sign codes

1 = mass	2 = mass & microcalcification
3 = spiculated mass	4 = spiculated mass & microcalcification
5 = microcalcification	6 = stellate
7 = stellate & microcalcification	8 = asymetrical density
9 = none	

Radiology confidence codes

1 = normal	2 = benign
3 = equivocal	4 = suspicious, probably malignant
5 = malignant	9 = not requested

Breast Ultrasound

Name of radiologist	. . . .	
Hospital	. . . .	
Date of report	........./....../.......	
Side	Right	Left
Ultrasound sign	. . . .	
Ultrasound confidence	. . . .	

Ultrasound codes

1 = normal	2 = cyst
3 = circumscribed mass with no attenuation	

4 = circumscribed mass with attenuation
5 = shadowing alone 6 = not done

Ultrasound confidence codes
1 = normal   2 = benign
3 = equivocal   4 = suspicious, probably malignant
5 = malignant   9 = not requested

Overall radiological opinion   Right.......... Left ....
1 = normal   2 = benign
3 = equivocal   4 = suspicious, probably malignant
5 = malignant

Other imaging
Chest x-ray   . . . .
Other x-rays   . . . .
Ultrasound liver   . . . .
Bone scan   . . . .
1 = no malignant abnormality   2 = malignancy   9 = not requested

4. PATHOLOGY

(This is based on a form currently in use in South Thames West)

Cytology
Name of Laboratory ....
Pathologist   ....
Date of report   ..../....../.......

Side   Right .... Left ....
Cytology result   . . . .
Codes
0 = not done   C2 = benign   C4 = suspicious
C1 = insufficient   C3 = prob benign   C5 = malignant

Histology
Name of laboratory ....
Pathologist   ....
Date of report   ..../....../.......

Codes
MALIGNANT - non-invasive or micro-invasive component
1 = DCIS: papillary   5 = LCIS:
2 = DCIS: cribriform   6 = Pagets disease
3 = DCIS: comedo
4 = DCIS: other

MALIGNANT - invasive
1 = Invasive ductal carcinoma   4 = Medullary
2 = Tubular or cribriform   5 = Mucoid
3 = Lobular invasive   6 = Other (specify)
Diagnosis codes:
1 = Normal   2 = Benign   3 = Malignant

Side: Right   Left
BENIGN   Y / N
MALIGNANT - Non-invasive or
Micro-invasive component type:

Grade if DCIS   . . . . (High / Low)
Microinvasion   . . . . (Y / N)
Max diameter   ....mm   ....mm
MALIGNANT - invasive component
type:

Multicentric   . . . . (Y / N)
Max diameter   ....mm   ....mm
Grade (1,2 or 3)   . . . .
Vascular invasion present. . . . . . (Y / N)
Axillary nodes present . . . . (Y / N)
Number positive: . . . .
Number negative: . . . .
Excision complet ed   . . . . (Y / N)
Distance   ....mm   ....mm

Diagnosis

5 LOCATION AND CLASSIFICATION OF MALIGNANCY

Location:

Location of lesion				Right	Left

Codes:

AX	C	IH	OH	LH	UH
LIQ	LOQ	UIQ	UOQ	SAR	

Classification:

1 = Operable   2 = Locally advanced inoperable
3 = Metastatic   4 = Patient unsuitable for surgery

6 COMMUNICATION OF DIAGNOSIS & TREATMENT PLANNING

How many hospital visits up to and including communication of diagnosis?..........

Date patient informed of cancer ..../...../.......

Was the diagnosis communicated by a consultant or fully trained specialist?..........
Was the patient seen by a breast cancer nurse specialist?...........................
                                                                 1 = No   2 = Yes
Name of breast cancer nurse specialist ....
Was the diagnosis discussed at a multi-professional review meeting?................
                                                                 1 = No   2 = Yes
Date treatment options discussed with patient   ..../..../......
by a consultant or fully trained specialist?   ..../..../......
by a breast cancer nurse specialist   ..../..../......
                                                                 1 = No   2 = Yes
If mastectomy planned give indications ....
1 = not performed   6 = multifocal tumour
2 = patient choice   7 = positive margins
3 = large tumour   8 = other clinical
4 = central tumour   9 = not specified
5 = extensive DCIS

Patient response
1 = not interested in reconstruction
2 = would like reconstruction (immediate or delayed)
3 = not relevant

7 TREATMENT - SURGERY

First surgical procedure: . . . . Date........./..../......
Breast procedure   . . . . Axillary procedure . . . .
Reconstruction: . . . .
Name of Surgeon: . . . .
Second surgical procedure: . . . . Date........./..../......
Breast procedure   . . . . Axillary procedure . . . .
Reconstruction: . . . .
Name of Surgeon: . . . .
Third surgical procedure: . . . . Date........./..../......
Breast procedure   . . . . Axillary procedure . . . .
Reconstruction: . . . .
Name of Surgeon: . . . .
Surgical codes

Breast procedure: . . . . Axillary procedure: . . . .

1 = Incision biopsy   1 = Sampling / Level 1 clearance

2 = Excision biopsy / lumpectomy   2 = Clearance to level 11 or 111

3 = Wide local excision   9 = None

4 = Segmentectomy / quandrantectomy

5 = Subcutaneous mastectomy (no skin removed / nipple preserved)

6 = Simple mastectomy (no muscle removed)

7 = Radical mastectomy

9 = None

Reconstruction?   . . . .
                    1 = None planned   2 = Immediate   3 = Delayed

Reconstruction procedure codes:

1 = with implant   2 = with tissue expansion   3 = TRAM flam

4 = TRAM flap   5 = TRAM flap with expansion   6 = LD flap

7 = LD flap with implant   8 = LD flap with expansion   9 = None

8 TREATMENT - ADJUVANT THERAPIES

Date of referral to oncologist   ..../..../......

Date first seen by oncologist   ..../..../......

Radiotherapy?   NO .... YES ....

Reason   ....

Treatment fields   ....

1 = Not clinically recommended   1 = Breast / chest wall

2 = Patient declined   2 = Axilla /gland fields

3 = In trial, randomised not to receive   3 = Combined (eg breast and axilla)

Date commencement of radiotherapy   ..../..../......

Systemic adjuvant therapy?

Endocrine Therapy   NO .... YES ....

Reason   ....

Treatment   ....

1 = Not clinically recommended   1 = Tamoxifen

2 = Patient declined   2 = Zoladex

3 = In trial, randomised not to receive   3 = Other (Specify).....................

Date of commencement of endocrine therapy   ..../..../......

Planned duration 2 yrs / 5 yrs

Chemotherapy   NO .... YES ....

Reason   ....

Date commencement of chemotherapy   ..../..../......

1 = Not clinically recommended

2 = Patient declined

3 = In trial, randomised not to receive

Clinical Trials

Has the patient been entered into a trial?

    NO .... YES ....

Reason   ....

Name of Trial   ....

1 = Not suitable   1 = CRC Under 50s

2 = Patient declined   2 = Zeneca Zebra

3 = Clinician unwilling   3 = CRC Over 50s

4 = CRC Chemotherapy   5 = aTTom

6 = UK DCIS   7 = BASO 11

8 = UKCCCR ABC   9 = other

9 FOLLOW-UP / OUTCOME

Date first seen in clinic post-operatively ..../..../......
Post-operative complications ....
1 = None   4 = Infection
2 = Haematoma   5 = Other (specify)....................................
3 = Seroma

Date of follow-up clinic ..../..../......
Significant morbidity ....
1 = None significant   6 = Numb upper inner arm
2 = Poor cosmetic result of conservation   7 = Stiff or frozen shoulder
3 = Chest wall pain   8 = Irradiation rib fracture, ulcer or lung fibrosis
4 = Lymphoedema   9 = Plexus neuropathy
5 = Breast oedema   10 = Other
Has treatment deviated from plan?..............
    1 = No   2 = Yes
If yes, state reason ....
Patient disease free? ....
    1 = No   2 = Yes
    3 = Possible recurrence

Date of first local recurrence ..../..../......
(breast / chest wall)
Date of first regional recurrence ..../..../......
axilla / SCF
Date of first contralateral disease ..../..../......
Date of first distant metastases ..../..../......
Site of first distant metastases ....
    1 = Bone   2 = Lung   3 = Liver   4 = Brain   5 = Other

Date of new primary non-breast tumour ..../..../......
Follow-up ceased? ....
    1 = No   2 = Yes
Reason follow-up ceased...
1 = Deceased   4 = Moved out of district
2 = Lost to follow-up   9 = Unknown
3 = Under care of GP
Date of death ..../..../......

Cause of death   . . . .

2 = Not due to breast cancer, but breast cancer present

3 = Not due to breast cancer, no breast cancer present

9 = Unknown

APPENDIX 3

Minimum Data Set for Cancer Registries as required in EL (92) 95

Patient Demographics:

Name ....

Address ....

....

Postcode ....

Sex ....

Date of Birth ....../..../......

Date of Death ....../..../......

Marital Status ....

NHS Number ....

Previous Surname (for record linkage)

Disease Specific ....

Site of primary growth ....

Side ....

Type and behaviour of growth ....

Record, type and registration details ....

Multiple tumour and death - certificate only indicators ....

Basis of diagnosis ....

Treatment ....

....

Stage and grade (breast and cervix only) ....

Screening data is only optional at present, as are occupation and ethnicity

References and Bibliography

Aspley S J   Implementation of ISO 9002 in cancer care;   International Jour of Health Care Quality Assurance; 9/2(1996) 28-30

Atkins H et al   Treatment of early breast cancer; a report after 10 years of a clinical trial; Br Med Jour 1972: 2: 423-9

Axelson C K et al   Axillary dissection on level 1 and 11 lymph nodes is important in breast cancer classification: Eur Jour Cancer 1992: 28A: 1415-18

Baker R   Problem solving with audit in general practice   Br Med Jour 1990; Vol 300 ; 326-8

Barera M   Distinction between social support concepts, measures and models   American Journal of Community Psychology 1986: Vol 14 (4): 413-415.

BASO   BASO Breast Unit Database Manual: Developed by Clatterbridge Centre for Oncology1996

Bastone G & Edwards M   Professional roles in providing evidence based practice   Br Jour of Health Care Management 1996 Vol 2;No 3

Baum M & Colletta A   Breast Cancer: A revolutionary concept Breast Cancer: Vol 2 No 1:April 1995

Baum M   Quack cancer cures or scientific remedies Journal of the Royal Society of Medicine 1996: 89 543-547

BBG   Provision of breast services in the UK; the advantages of specialist breast units; Report of a working party of the British Breast Group1994

Berwick D M , Enthoven A, & Bunker J P   Quality management in the NHS; the doctors role; Br Med Jour   Vol 304 25th Jan 1992

Black N & Thompson C Obstacles to medical audit; British doctors speak. Social Science Medicine1993; Vol 36; 849-856

Boud D   Developing autonomy: Wiley1985

Buxton M   Achievements of audit in the NHS. Quality of Health Care 1994 Vol 3(supp) 35-36.

Calman K Hospital doctors training for the future 1995

Chamberlain J et al   National Health service Breast Screening Programme Results for 1991-1992: Br Med Jour 1993 Vol 307; 353-6

Cobb S Social support as a moderator of life stressors Psychosomatic Medicine Vol 38: 1976: 300-14

Crombie I K & HTO Davies   Towards good audit   Br Jour of Hospital Medicine 1992: Vol 48 No: 3 182-185

Culyer A EL/94/48 NHSE 1994

Curley P J et al   Audit of vascular surgical workload; use of data for service development: Ann. R. Coll. Surg. Engl. 1996: Vol 98: 209-213

Current Trials Working Party of the Cancer Research Campaign; Breast cancer Trials Group: Preliminary results from the Cancer Research Campaign Trial evaluating Tamoxifen duration in women aged fifty years or older with breast cancer: Jour of the National Cancer Institute: Vol 88 No 24; Dec 18:1996

Dakof G A & Taylor ST Victims perceptions of social support; what is helpful for whom? Jour of Personality and Social Psychology 1990 58(1) 80-91

Davies C et al Factors influencing audit in general practice International Jour of Health Care Quality Assurance 9/5 (1996) 5-9

Davies D.A;Thompson M.A; Oxman AD & Hayes RB Changing physician performance: A systematic review of the effect of continuing medical education strategies JAMA; 1995 Sept 6: 274 700-705

Deans G T et al An audit of surgery of the parotid gland Ann R Coll Surg Engl 1995; 77: 188-192

Delay T S The inter-relationship between coping and social support in breast cancer patients and their spouses: Paper presented at the meeting of Current Concepts in Psycho-Oncology; I.V Memorial Sloan-Kettering Cancer Centre N.Y 1995

DoH Working for Patients HMSO 1989

DoH Specialist Medical Training HMSO1992

DoH A guide to specialist registrar training HMSO1996

DoH Clinical audit; meeting and improving the standards in health care D.O.H: London 1993.

DoH Methods to promote the implementation of research findings in the NHS; priorities for evaluation: DoH 1995

DoH R & D priorities in relation to the interface between primary and secondary care: Report to the NHS Central Research and Development Committee; DoH 1994

DoH Research and development in the new NHS: Functions and responsibilities: NHSE: sept 1995

Devlin B Comment Ann R Coll Surg Engl 1996: 78: 410-411

Donabedian A The quality of care; how can it be assessed; JAMA 260 1988: 1743-8

Dorrell S Evolving health care: Br Jour of Hospital Medicine 1996 Vol 56: No 4

Dunkel-Schetter C Social support and cancer: findings based on patient interviews and their implications; Jour of Social Issues 1984: Vol 40 (4) 77-98

Elal- Lawrence G & Celikoglu P Social support and psychological well being in breast cancer patients: Health & Social Care in the Community 1995 3: 1-7

Fisher B, Anderson S, & Redmond C K et al Re-analysis and results after 12 years of follow up in a randomised clinical trial comparing total mastectomy with lumpectomy with or without intervention in the treatment of breast cancer. New Engl Jour Med: 1995: 333: 1456-611996

Firth-Cozens J & Storer D: Registrars and Senior Registrars perceptions of their audit activities: Quality in Health Care: 1992: 1: 161-4

Garvigan L A breast cancer clinical audit strategy for South Thames: a consultation document produced by the South Thames Breast Cancer Clinical Audit Advisory Committee The Health Care Evaluation Unit;Report no. 9:St George's Hospital

GIVIO Investigators Impact of follow up testing on survival and health related quality of life in breast cancer patients: A multi centre randomised controlled trial JAMA 1994: 271: 1587-92

Gordon C & Christensen J.P Health Telematics for clinical guidelines and protocols: IOS Press 19951994

Graham-Smith D Evidence based medicine: Socratic dissent: Br. Med Jour 1995: 310: 1126-7

Gillet R & Harrow J Management within the Medical research Council: Br Med Jour 1993 Vol 306: 1668-72

Gillet R & Harrow J Is medical research well served by peer review Br Med Jour 1993 306 1672-5

Grol R Research and development in quality of care: establishing the research agenda Quality in Health Care 1996; 235-242

Grundfield E et al Routine follow up of breast cancer in primary care; randomsied trial Br Med Jour 1996: 313: 665-9

Heinbuch S E Achieveing effective service contracting results: the process is the key to success: International Journal of Health Care Quality Assurance: 9/3 (1996) 32-41

Houle C O Continuing learrning in the professions Josey Bass Inc Publishers:1980 International Hospital Group Breast cancer information pack (Draft) NHS:South Thames June 1996

Jones A Adjuvant treatment in high risk breast cancer Br Jour of Hospital Medicine 1996: Vol 55 No 4

Kerrison S, Packwood T & Buxton M Medical audit: taking stock Kings Fund Centre: London 1993

Kemple T J & Hayter S R Audit of diabetes in general practice Br Med Jour 1991 Vol 302: 451-3

Kerr DNS et al Continuing medical education: experience and opinions of consultants: Br Med Jour 1993 Vol 306: No 1 1398-1402

Kumar F & Brown A Quality of Health 1992

Long A and Harrison S Managers Checklist: Health Service Journal: Health management Guide: 1995

May N & Pope C Rigour and qualitative research Br Med Jour: Vol 311 8th July 1995

McKee C M Can audit be implemented by 1991? Postgrad Med Jour 1989 Vol 65: 645-9

Marsh S K & Archer T J Accuracy of general practitioner referrals to a breast clinic: Ann R Coll Surg Engl; 1996 Vol 78: 203-205

Meyerowitz B Psycho-social correlates of breast cancer and its treatment Psychological Bulletin 1980 : Vol 87 (1): 108-31

NHSE & Greenhalgh & Co Ltd Clinical Audit and operational clinical research: HMSO1996

NHSE Promoting Clinical Effectivness: DoH 1996

Melville A et al Management of primary breast cancer Quality of Health Care 1996: Vol 5: 250-258

Orr E Open communication as an effective stress management method for breast cancer patients: Jour of Human Stress 1986: 12 (4) 75-185

Owen P Clinical practice and medical research: bridging the divide between the cultures: Br Jour of General Practice 1995 Vol 45: 557-560

Rees L & Wass J Undergraduate medical education : Br Med Jour 1993 Vol 306 258-261

Revans J   Action Learning   Routledge 1980

Robinson S Audit in the therapy professions: some constraints on progress Quality in Health Care 1996; 5: 206-214

Rosenberg W & Donald A Evidence -based medicine; an approach to clinical problem solving BMJ 1995:310 (6987) 1122-26

Rosselli del Turco M et al Intensive diagnostic follow up after treatment of primary breast cancer; A randomised trial JAMA1994;271 : 1593-7

Royal College of Surgeons in England Guideleines to Clinical Audit: 1996

Sackett D L & Haynes R.B On the need for evidence based medicine: Evidence Based Medicine 1995 1(1): 5-6

Sainsbury R et al Influence of clinician workload and patterns of treatment on survival from breast cancer: Lancet 1995 :345: 1265-70

Saunders C M & Baum M Quality of life during treatment for cancer Br Jour of Hospital medicine 1992 Vol 48 No 2

Savage S A & Clarke V A Factors associated with screening mammography and breast self examination intentions Health Education Research Vol 11 No 4 1996: 409-421

Schipper H; Turley E.A; Baum M A new framework for cancer research
The Lancet Vol 384, October 26, 1996

Schon D. A The reflective practitioner; New York: Basic Books 1983

Schrijvers C T M et al Deprivation and survival from breast cancer   Br Jour of Cancer 1995 Vol 75 738-743

Scott P Auditing our brave new world   Horizons October 1989

Shaw C D Medical audit: a hospital handbook 1990a Kings Fund Centre : London

Shaw C D   Criterion based audit: Br Med Jour 1990b Vol 300 649-651

Shaw C D & Costain D W Guidelines for medical audit; seven principles: Br Med Jour 1989 Vol 299: 498-499

Sitges-Serva A Research during higher surgical training; a luxury or a must: Ann R Coll Surg Engl 1995 Vol 77: 1-2

Skidmore F D UK Cancer Registry statistics; can the partially sighted lead the blind: European Journal of Surgical Oncology 1996: Vol 22: 467-468 1994

Smith T   Medical audit: closing the feedback loop is essential Br Med Jour 1990 Vol 300: 65

Swales J D Priorities in medical research   Br Jour of Hosp Med 1996 Vol 56

Taylor S E et al Social support, support groups and the cancer patient Jour of Consulting and Clinical Psychology 1986 Vol 54 (5) 608-15

Thames Cancer Registry   Cancer in South East of England 1991 Thames Cancer Registry: Sutton (1994)

Thompson R.G & Barton A Is audit running out of steam? Quality in Health Care 1994; Vol 3 ;225-229

Wakefield S E & Powis J A Benign breast surgery: is there a need for out-patient follow up? An R Coll Surg Engl: 1995 77; 457-459

Williams O   What is clinical audit?   Ann R Coll Surg Engl: 1996: 78; 406-411

Wortman C. B   Social support and the cancer patient; conceptual issues and the methodological issues: Cancer 1984 Vol 53; 2339-60

Index

ABAB type studies   18, 29
action based research   1
audit
  definitions 2
  essential elements   4
  functions   1,2,6,7,19,40
  history   8,24
  processes   3, 9
  cycle   11
  key criteria   10
  interpretation 10
  questions about   13
  types   20
  differences between   22
age characteristics   61,62
annual figures   57
ANOVA   54
Aspley S J   2

Baker R   12
BASO   15,17
Barera M 80
Baum M & Colletta A   42
Baum M   42
breast surgery   59, 60
  -volume by cases 59
  -consultant workload   59
  -hospital workload 59
breast conserving surgery
  see breast surgery
Boud D   41
British Breast Group   15,17,25
Buxton M   2

Calman Enquiry   34, 40
cancers
  -types 65-67

-ductal 65-67
- lobular 65-67
- tubular 65-67
-invasive 68
-non -invasive 68
cancer treatment   69-74
  -chemotherapy 69-70
  -radiotherapy   69-70
  -mastectomy   69-70
  causes of death   75
Centre for Research Dissemination (CRD)   81
Certificate of Completion of Specialist
Training 36
Chamberlain J et al   64
Clinical outcomes Group   25,26
Clinical Trials Co-ordinator 46-51
cohorts
  -cohort 1   43
  -cohort 2   47,62
  Cobb S   80
Crombie I K et al   12,15,16
Cochrane Centre   38
counselling   79
Culyer A   30
Curley P J et al   17,18

Dakof G A & Taylor S T   80
data recording   82
data sets
  -MDS Cancer Registries   44
  -BAS0   44
  -Garvigan L 44
  -Worthing   44
  -recorded   48
data analysis   53
  -initial considerations 53
Davies D A et al   2
Deans   G T et al   18
Delay T S   79

Devlin B   17,24
DoH   4
  Working Group on Specialist Medical
  Training   35
Donabedian A   15
Ductal Carcinoma in -situ DCIS   64
Dunkel-Schetter C   80,81
Elal-Lawrence G & Celikoglu P   80
Evidence Based Medicine   31,37,38,40
experiential Learning   41

Fallowfield L   80
Firth-Cozens J & Storer D   5

Garvigan L   15
Gordon C   2

Health of the Nation figures   58
histological analysis   65
Houle C O   39
hypothetico-deductive approach   42

Incidence   64
ISO 9002   2

Kemple I J & Hayter S R   15
Kerrison S, Packwood T & Buxton M   5
Kumar R & Brown A   7

Langlands A 27
Long A & Harrison S   38

McKee C M et al   12, 16
Melville A et al 81
Meyerowitz B   80

National Audit Office   10
NHSE & Greenhalgh & Co 3,5,14
NHS & Community Care Act 1990 ,
23,34,37,60
NHSE   26
  - R & D Structure 30-34
  - Research & Development Directorate   30

Open communication   80
Orr E   80

patient volume   55
practice implications   63
professionalisation   39
psychological support
  functions of 79—82
  sources of 70

Quality Assurance   4

R eid   17
research based knowledge   42
reflection on practice 40-42
  see reflective practice   83
Robinson S   4,5
Rosenberg W & Donaldson A 38
Revans J   12

Sackett D L   16,37
Schon D   41
Scott P   10
Screen detected cases   55,61
Self directed learning   39
Shaw C   12,15
Shaw C & Costain D W 12
Smith T   12
South Thames   56
Specialist nurses   82
Spread sheet headings   50
Symptomatic cases   54-55
Summary of findings   76

Thames Cancer Registry Statistics   64
Thompson R G & Barton A 5

West Sussex Breast Centre 53,56
Williams O   2,12,17, 21, 24, 28, 29
Wortman   C B   80